How To Write
and _Sell_
Your Personal
Experiences

OTHER BOOKS BY LOIS DUNCAN

Nonfiction:
Chapters: My Growth as a Writer

Novels:
The Twisted Window
Locked in Time
The Third Eye
Stranger with My Face
Daughters of Eve
Killing Mr. Griffin
Summer of Fear
Down a Dark Hall
I Know What You Did Last Summer
Ransom
They Never Came Home
    and others

Juveniles:
A Gift of Magic
Hotel for Dogs
Major Andre, Brave Enemy
Silly Mother
Giving Away Suzanne
The Littlest One in the Family

Children's Verse:
Horses of Dreamland
From Spring to Spring
The Terrible Tales of Happy Days School

Lullaby Cassette (audio):
Songs From Dreamland

Educational Cassette for Use in Schools (video):
A Visit with Lois Duncan
The video and audio cassettes are produced by RDA
Enterprises, 1112 Dakota N.E., Albuquerque, NM 87110

How to Write and Sell Your Personal Experiences

by Lois Duncan

Cincinnati, Ohio

How to Write and Sell Your Personal Experiences. Copyright ©
1979 by Lois Duncan. Revised, second edition copyright © 1986 by
Lois Duncan. Printed in the United States of America. All rights re-
served. No part of this book may be reproduced in any form or by
any electronic or mechanical means including information storage
and retrieval systems without permission in writing from the publisher, except by a reviewer who may quote brief passages in a review. Published by Writer's Digest Books, an imprint of F&W Publications, Inc., 1507 Dana Avenue, Cincinnati, Ohio 45207. Second
edition.
Second printing, 1982
Third printing, 1984
First paperback printing, 1986
Second paperback printing, 1987

Library of Congress Cataloging in Publication Data

Duncan, Lois, 1934-
   How to write and sell your personal experiences.
   Includes index.
   1. Authorship. I. Title.
PN147.D8   808'.025   79-17407
ISBN 0-89879-223-1

The following page is an extension of this copyright page.

For Don

Acknowledgments

I would like to thank—

my students and former students for allowing me to cite their work as examples;

those writer and editor friends whose words of wisdom I have quoted;

and my editors, Carol Cartaino and Elizabeth MacCallum, for their helpful suggestions as this book was being written.

LDA

Contents

How to Write
and _Sell_
Your Personal
Experiences

Introduction

Did you ever answer the telephone to hear a strange voice announce that you had just won $1,500?

I did. It was a number of years ago, but it seems like yesterday that I received a call informing me that I had been awarded the Grand Prize in the *Writer's Digest* Creative Writing Contest. Soon after the check arrived, the editor called again, this time to request a photograph of me at the typewriter to run on the cover of the magazine.

Then letters of protest began to arrive.

"It's not fair," wrote a furious man from Columbus, Ohio. "This woman is a professional writer. I am a real estate agent with a family to support. I don't have the cash to spend on expensive writing courses. How can I be expected to compete with someone who does?"

A woman from Memphis, Tennessee, wrote, "Professional writers should be barred from this contest. They have access to resources the rest of us do not. They have the freedom to travel and interview famous people, to go to the scene of exciting events, and to get to know editors on a first-name basis Average people like myself, tied at home with housework and small children, don't stand a chance."

There was even a letter from an English professor at our local university. "I encouraged my creative writing students to enter this contest," he wrote. "I never would have done this if I had realized professionals would be allowed to enter."

The publisher of *Writer's Digest* responded to these letters with the reasonable observation that writing is a field in which all of us—the published and the unpublished, the author of a first story and of a five hundredth—compete on the same level. The product stands on its own feet, regardless of who wrote it, and the market is open to everyone. (This was proven the following year when the winner of the Grand Prize was an unpublished writer.) Things simmered down, and eventually the protesters drifted back to their typewriters to put them to more productive use.

My photograph was never published. I like to think this was because the editors were reluctant to stir up any further reader reaction and not because they suddenly discovered I wore bifocals and had an overbite.

That incident left me with a question: Just what do people think a "professional writer" is—someone who hails from a different planet? Why would a real-estate salesman from Ohio feel threatened by having to compete with *me*? Why would college students feel overshadowed by someone with less education than they have? Why would a Memphis housewife immediately assume that I have more access to salable material than she does?

Writers are real people. You don't have to breathe special air to be one. The truth was, my prize-winning story had been written in bits and pieces during children's naptimes. I had not had to "travel and interview famous people" in order to write it. I had only to reach within myself. My story was a first-person account of the death of my mother.

I was at that time a totally homebound writer. Married at nineteen, I had had no formal training in writing beyond what I had received in a public high school. I lived in Albu-

querque, New Mexico, not exactly the "in spot" for hobnob-
bing with editors. My husband, Don Arquette, was an electri-
cal engineer at Sandia Laboratories. We had four and two-
thirds children: Robin, fifteen; Kerry, thirteen; Brett, ten; and
Donnie, three. Kate was due to be born in another three
months. Days at our house started with a chaotic family
breakfast at 7:00 a.m. and ended when Donnie had been
walked to the bathroom, the teenagers had been dragged
from the telephone, and the last escaped hamster had been
located and recaged.

The following summer, I was invited to lecture at a writers'
conference at the University of California. Robin went along
for the ride. When we returned, she announced to the family,
"I couldn't believe it! Mother made speeches, and people
took notes, just like she was somebody important! After that,
they all went crowding up to talk to her, and everybody wanted to sit next to her at dinner!"

The rest of the clan regarded her in stunned silence.

Finally Brett said, "I hope you didn't give it away. I hope
you didn't tell them that back home she's just an ordinary
mother."

Professional writers are ordinary people. There may be a
few who live exotic lives, but the great majority does not.
They get up in the morning when the alarm goes off and rub
the sleep out of their eyes and go stumbling down the stairs,
trying to remember where they put the filters for the coffee-
pot, just like everybody else.

Which raises the inevitable second question: Just what do
"ordinary people" find to write about that is interesting
enough so that editors are willing to buy their stories?

That one was answered for me when I was thirteen years
old.

I grew up in Sarasota, Florida, and started submitting stories to magazines when I was ten, painstakingly pecking
them out on my mother's portable typewriter and shipping
them off to such publications as *The Saturday Evening Post*,
Esquire and *The New Yorker*. I looked up the addresses in the
magazines on my parents' coffee table. Needless to say, my

manuscripts were returned to me quickly. (I did receive some encouragement from an editor at *Ladies' Home Journal* who wrote a note on her rejection slip suggesting that I "try us again in ten years.")

Rather than curtailing further submissions, those rejections stirred me on to a frenzy of activity. My efforts became more and more ambitious. Tales of flaming romance, blood-spurting violence, pain and passion, lust and adventure, flew back and forth between Florida and New York in a steady stream. My parents thought me cute and funny. My teachers thought me horrid and precocious. As for myself, I was proud. While my schoolmates were picking up jacks and trading comic books, I—plump, bespectacled and unimpressive as I might appear—was plunging ahead toward the glamorous career that would make me immortal.

Three years passed, and I accumulated so many rejection slips that my mother made me stop saving them. "After all, dear, when you've read one, you've read them all."

Then one day I came home from school to find a craggy-faced giant of a man visiting with my parents. He was a new neighbor who had just moved in down the beach from us. He was also a writer whose name was MacKinlay Kantor.

"Lois," my father said after introductions had been made, "why don't you show Mr. Kantor the story that came back yesterday from *The Saturday Evening Post?*"

He did not have to ask twice. What an opportunity! A real published author was trapped right there in our living room! I rushed to get the story and stood expectantly at his elbow as Mr. Kantor scanned the pages.

The praise I was so eagerly awaiting was not served up to me.

"My dear," Mr. Kantor exploded, "this is pure shit!"

It was the first time that word had been used in my presence. My mother was as shocked as I was.

"Mack!" she said reprovingly. "Lois is only thirteen!"

"I don't care *how* old she is!" bellowed the man who was later to become my friend and mentor. "If she is putting her stories into the market and expects someone to buy them, she is old enough to be realistic. What kind of subject matter is this for a kid? She has never had a love affair or seen a man get murdered. Good writing comes from the heart, not off the top of the head."

He turned to me and added more gently, "Throw this stuff in the trash, child, and go write a story about something you know about. Write something that rings true."

I was crushed. I was also challenged. Later that week I did write a story about a fat, shy little girl with braces and glasses who covered her insecurity by writing stories about imaginary adventures. I submitted it to a teen publication called *Calling All Girls*, and by return mail I received a check for $25.

It was the most incredible moment of my life.

My fate was sealed. From then on, I wrote about what I knew about and could hardly wait to rush home from school each day to fling myself at the typewriter. I poured the pain and joy of adolescence on to page after page. My first kiss, my first heartbreak, my first deep theological discussion with a boy whose religion was different from my own, all became subjects for stories. When I wasn't invited to Carol Johnson's slumber party, I wiped away my tears and wrote about it. When I lost the lead in the class play to Barbara Werner, I wrote a story in which I *got* the lead. I flooded the teen magazines with manuscripts, and despite the unpolished writing, the gut reality of the material carried them over the line, and a surprising number of them sold.

At sixteen, I won second prize in *Seventeen* magazine's annual short-story contest. At seventeen, I won third prize, and at eighteen, I took first prize and used the money to get married. My greatest triumph was the sale of my home economics report. I was the only girl in the history of Sarasota High School who ever flunked home ec. Lost in daydreams, I forgot to knot my thread and hemmed my skirt all semester long, working my way round and round the circle of material, drawing the thread smoothly along an endless path. When the end-of-the-year fashion show was held, I was not allowed to participate, but I wrote up the whole sad tale and sold it for

$50. With that, I bought a skirt that was perfectly beautiful. Whenever anyone asked me where I got it, I humbly said, "Home ec."

And so it has been with me as time has passed. For all these many years, I have continued to write from the heart about the things I know about, the people I care about, the feelings with which I am most familiar. I have written about love and loss, divorce and remarriage, the birth of babies, the rearing of children, the transitions a woman makes at the natural turning points of her life.

Few of my life's experiences have been wasted. When Donnie landed in a dermatologist's office after a family camping trip, I wrote "Mid-Summer Myths," which dealt with outdated beliefs about poison ivy. When Kerry and I worked as extras in a locally filmed western, I wrote up the experience for *Girl Talk*. When Brett was arrested for smoking pot in a high school parking lot, I wrote a "My Problem" piece for *Good Housekeeping*. While struggling to help a child with learning problems make it through middle school, I wrote articles about learning disabilities for *Ladies' Home Journal*, *Impact*, *Working Mother*, *Current Health*, *Woman's Day*, *Living With Teenagers*, and *Marriage and Family Living*.

Little of the material of which my stories and articles are fashioned is exciting or sensational. It is as available to you as it is to me. People find it interesting because they can relate to it. People are more interested in *people* than in anything else in the world.

There is a fairy tale I used to read to Kate when she was little about a girl who was taught by an elf the secret of spinning straw into gold. I like to think of writers like myself as resembling that girl. We, too, use the basic "straw" of our experiences to create something of value. It is the same straw that lies about everywhere; it isn't imported from the Orient. All of us have piles of it at our disposal, ready and waiting to be reaped from the lawns of our lives. But sometimes it takes a little direction to know exactly what to do with it in order to transform it into golden cloth.

Step by step, since my first sale so many years ago, I have

moved into a writing career that has given me great joy and satisfaction. Not everybody is lucky enough to have a Pulitzer Prize-winning author to point the way. Sometimes we have to settle for whatever "elf" is at hand.

I am at hand.

I hope I can help.

... the pain and joy of adolescence poured on to page after page ...

I met Roger in the orthodontist's office. Now I think back on it, that might have been what put the damper on our whole relationship. Perhaps in my subconscious mind I connected him with wires and mouth rinses and wads of cotton. . . .

("A Gift from Roger," *American Girl*, 1960)

. . . Anne enters her room, and she is not beautiful anymore. She is only a plump little girl in a tight blue formal, with too much lipstick on her mouth.

The dog, Turvey, looking guilty, gets off the pillow and quickly moves to the foot of the bed. Anne throws herself down beside him and buries her face against his back and begins to cry.

"Oh, Turvey," she sobs. "I'm *fat!*"

("The Last Night," *Seventeen*, 1953)

. . . It was night now, but not really dark because of the lights from the houses and the street lights, and the eleven maple trees were huge dark masses against the night. I walked quickly, not bothering to count them. This time I knew I wasn't going to walk casually past the Tutter house. There was an ache inside me, almost too great to bear, and I knew I had to see Joe. It didn't matter if he thought I was completely crazy. I had to see him or I'd die. . . .

("Stop Calling Me Baby," *Seventeen*, 1962)

. . . And I managed it. It is a little shameful to me now to think about how schemingly I managed it—a smile here, a sideways look there. "Hi, Ted," every time I passed him in the hall. "What page did she say we were to do tonight, Ted?" as we left class and happened to reach the door together. A week or two of that and then the big step. "Nancy's having a party this weekend, Ted, a girl-ask-boy affair. Would you like to go?" It was really pretty easy.

Ted was standing at his locker when I asked him. He had the door open and was fishing out his gym shorts, and when he turned he looked surprised, as though he were sure he had not heard me correctly.

"Go? You mean with you?"

("Written in the Stars," *Seventeen*, 1959)

. . . Before, Kathy had been a friend, but now suddenly she was a friend no longer.

"I have a cousin," she said coldly, "who has terrible buck teeth like yours, Jane. The dentist thinks she should have braces. You've had braces so many years—do they feel as awkward as they look?"

("The Wish," *American Girl*, 1957)

. . . That was all. There was nothing to say, nothing to do. She saw him at the pond several times after, alone at first, and then with several different girls. The hurt really came when it was one special girl, over and over again. Marilyn watched them sometimes as they circled the pond together. The girl was an even worse skater than Marilyn, but she was cute and unattached and she laughed a lot, and her admiring brown eyes said that there was no other boy in the world but Jack and that he was wonderful.

("The Silver Bracelet," *Seventeen*, 1952)

The most reliable vehicles for your personal experiences

1. The Best Bets

Few people lack practice in writing about their experiences. That is what we do routinely in personal letters. We write to our parents, our in-laws, our children, and our out-of-town friends, and fill them in on what's going on in our lives.

We recognize, however, that the same things are not of interest to everyone, and we do not write to all our correspondents in the same way. My mother-in-law might be thrilled to receive a six-page epistle detailing the antics and achievements of her adorable grandchildren, but a business acquaintance would not. A writer friend might be interested in learning about a turnover of editors at a major publishing house, but an interior decorator friend would find such information boring.

Just as we do not pour identical material into all of our letters, we do not always use the same format. There are particular forms that are appropriate for different types of letters. A business letter is written differently from a condolence letter; a love letter will bear little resemblance to the bread-and-butter note we write our hostess after a dinner party.

These same truths apply to an even greater degree when we begin to write for possible publication. We are now facing a problem of pleasing not only those people who already know us, but also those people to whom we are strangers. In our personal experience articles and stories, we will be drawing on much of the same raw material that we use in our personal letters, but before we set these experiences on paper we must make some decisions. How can the material be put to use most effectively? What type of people will find it most interesting? What form can we give it that will make it most meaningful?

Several months ago I received a letter from a friend who had just returned from a 600-mile bicycle tour of the Holy Lands. She thought, quite rightly, that this experience should be shared. She had written it up in the form of a log, starting with her farewell glimpse of her children as she and her husband pulled out of their driveway en route to the airport and continuing chronologically through the overseas flight, the assembly of the bicycles, her first impression of each of her tour companions, and each day's adventures, be they flat tires, sight-seeing treks, or dangerous attempts to navigate rain-slick mountain trails.

"Where do you think I should submit this?" she asked me.

I knew how much work had gone into her gathering of the material. At the same time, I felt dishonesty would be no kindness.

"I don't think you should submit it anywhere as it now stands," I said. "You need to decide first on what angle you want to take with this. You have the potential here for many different sorts of articles. Pick the one you want to write and mold your material to fit."

Here are some of the possibilities I suggested to her:

An article for a religious magazine. For this she would need to concentrate on describing the cities and countryside in view of the biblical events that had occurred at various locations.

An article for a bicycling magazine. This would be a "how-to" piece that would educate readers about how they too might experience such an adventure.

An article for a women's magazine. This would be the human interest story of a diminutive housewife who faced the greatest physical challenge of her life.

An article for an inspirational, family-centered magazine. Here she would emphasize the closeness she and her husband attained through sharing a memorable experience.

Once her article type was chosen, she would then need to select from her log appropriate material with which to construct the piece. She would not just throw in everything. In a religious article, there would be no place for a detailed account of the technical problems involved in assembling the bicycle, though for a bicycling publication that would be crucial. For a bicycling magazine, she would not write about the psychological problems a mother faces when she is separated from her children, an issue that would be well suited to a women's publication.

The trip might even provide her with background material for a fiction story or a novel, if she wishes to use it in that way. I think, though, that for the beginning writer who is making an initial attempt to break into print, the nonfiction article is the easiest starting point. Today's magazines publish far more fact than fiction, and the nonfiction door provides the easiest entrance to publication.

Certain types of articles are especially good vehicles for personal experiences:

The Personal Experience Piece in Its Purest Form. This is simply the written account of something you've experienced. The catch is that it must be an experience that will interest other people. It does not have to be startling or highly dramatic, as long as it is a story readers will relate to and find significant. In order to achieve this effect, you must shape the story so that it builds to a satisfying conclusion. The experience you describe should have taught you a lesson, given you a new viewpoint on life, helped you change something that needed changing, or made it possible for you to understand and accept a situation that could not be changed.

Here are some personal experience subjects that produced salable articles for students of mine at the University of New Mexico:

"The May-December Marriage—Can It Really Work?" by a twenty-six-year-old man who is happily married to a woman of fifty.

"The Day I Was Fired," by a middle-aged woman who suddenly lost the job she had held for twenty years.

"I Lost Sixty Pounds Through Yoga," by the skinniest kid I've ever seen.

"My Daughter, the Drug Addict," by a woman whose own experience as an alcoholic made it possible for her to help her teenage daughter overcome drug addiction.

"The Heartbreak of the Long Distance Mother," by a young woman who allowed her ex-husband to have custody of their child.

"Our Host the Ghost," by a girl who grew up in a haunted house.

"Loving Phil," by a girl who learned to adjust to her mother's remarriage.

"We Adopted a Live-in Grandpa," by a woman whose family took in an elderly friend to live with them on a permanent basis.

"But We Did It First," by an American Indian who wrote an article for a bow-hunting magazine about his adventures as a member of an all-Indian hunting club.

In the case of each of these stories, the author drew upon his or her life experiences to make a *definite point:*

That May-December marriages can work.
That being fired is not the end of the world.
That Yoga is a good way to lose weight.
That drug addicts can be helped to save themselves.

That the custody decision is not one to be made easily.
That ghosts do exist and can be fun to live with.
That learning to love a stepfather is worth the effort.
That grandfathers have an important place in family life.
That Indian bow-hunters know things that other hunters don't.

When writing their articles, these authors sifted through the ingredients of their personal experiences and utilized only those parts that built toward the conclusions they wanted the reader to reach. They carefully shaped their stories so that they did not just wander across the paper but led to a definite destination.

The Drama in Real Life Articles. It is amazing what people go through and live to tell—but not to write—about. If you as a writer can put into words the account of someone else's dramatic, true-life experience, you will find editors waiting for you with open arms.

The top market for this sort of story is *Reader's Digest*, with its "Drama in Real Life" series, but almost all magazines are receptive to this kind of material. There are stories all around you if you make yourself aware of them. Human beings survive fires, floods, and tornados; they apprehend burglars unarmed; they risk their lives for others; they find long-lost relatives; they face apparently insurmountable problems and overcome them. These things do not always happen somewhere else. They happen to the people in your life and mine. Almost everyone we meet has at least one good story lurking somewhere in a closet of his or her life. As writers, it's up to us to be continuously on the lookout for the chance remark with deeper implications.

One story of mine was the product of a comment dropped by a casual acquaintance at a cocktail party. "This is the first glass of wine I've had in a year," she said. "I can't keep liquor in the house because of Bobby."

"Because of *Bobby!*" I exclaimed. A clean-cut fifteen-year-old with an ingratiating grin, Bobby was my younger son's good buddy.

"He's an alcoholic," Bobby's mother said matter-of-factly. "For years I lived in terror that he would kill me during one of his drunken rages. Finally, thank God, I was able to get him into an alcoholic rehabilitation program. I went through the same thing with his older brother three years ago. Alcoholism runs in families, you know. The father of my sons is an alcoholic also. That's why I divorced him."

Anticipating a curt refusal, I hesitantly asked her how she would feel about having me write about the situation. Her response was one of gratitude. "Would you really be willing to? How wonderful! If I could share what I've learned about teenage alcoholism with other parents, I'd feel that all this misery has resulted in something positive."

Another good source of subject matter is your local newspaper. Keep an eye on the features; that's where human interest stories abound. Look for the heroic ("Elderly Woman Battles Mountain Lion to Protect Grandson"); the inspiring ("High School Athlete Donates Kidney to Sick Sister"); the tragic with an upbeat ending ("Mother Reunited with Kidnapped Daughter"). The heroes of such stories, having savored the sweet taste of local recognition, are usually delighted by the thought of achieving a second round of fame by being written up for a national magazine.

The Personality Piece. This is also called a profile. It is hard to find a magazine that does not run at least one personality piece per issue, and most use several. As I mentioned before, people are interested in people—in what they are like, in how they think, in what they do with their lives and why.

The majority of us don't have much chance to interview the nationally famous; Clint Eastwood doesn't jog through our neighborhood, and Jackie Onassis seldom rams her basket into ours at the supermarket. But there are thousands of little-known people who are unique in their own ways and would be of interest to readers of specific publications. A number of these may live right in your hometown.

An example: Donnie's first grade teacher, Lela Koster, taught with the aid of a homemade dollhouse. Her students learned about science by wiring the house for electricity, about math by making measurements as they built furniture, about reading and writing by composing their own reading charts to describe the construction process. They then made pipecleaner dolls to occupy the house and wrote and illustrated stories about the dolls' adventures.

I heard about the house from Donnie, who chattered about it constantly. I saw it for the first time at a PTA meeting. A light clicked on in my brain—"This is a story!" I interviewed Mrs. Koster, took pictures of the children involved in their sawing, wiring, and painting, and sold the story to an educational journal called *Teacher*.

How do you locate interesting personalities? It's hard *not* to find them if you keep your mind open and look around you. One of the nicest success stories I know concerns Bill Buchanan, whose children were always talking about their gym teacher, John Baker. Bill visited the kids' school and met Baker, finding him, indeed, an unusually dedicated and caring teacher. Two months later, Baker died of cancer.

Bill first wrote an article about John Baker for *Reader's Digest*. He then expanded the piece into a best-selling book, *A Shining Season*, which subsequently was filmed for television. Bill is a retired serviceman who decided in midlife that he would like to become a writer. He found ideal subject matter right under his nose in his children's schoolyard.

Do you know a "John Baker" whose life story is touching and inspirational? How about the members of your family? Sometimes we are so close to interesting people that we take them for granted and lose sight of the fact that to others they might be fascinating.

My student, Nanci, wrote an article about her widowed aunt. Nanci's uncle, who had worked for the narrow-gauge scenic railroad in Durango, Colorado, had been the breadwinner, while his wife stayed home to keep house and take care of nine children. Upon her husband's death, Nanci's aunt, who had never worked outside the home, had been suddenly faced with the awesome challenge of having to come up with some way to support ten people.

According to Nanci, she solved her problem by getting the whole family jobs with the railroad: one son as an engineer, one as fireman, two as track repairmen, and the girls as cooks and waitresses in restaurants catering to the tourist trade. Mom organized the household around the various conflicting schedules, preparing meals at odd times, sewing and laundering uniforms, and chauffeuring her children back and forth to their jobs. Working only the summer months, this enterprising family managed not only to earn enough to live on but also to put all the kids and Mom herself through college.

Good Housekeeping grabbed the story. It was a natural for them. Why hadn't it occurred to Nanci to write it before?

"I don't know," she said when I asked her. "I just didn't think about it. I mean, after all, we're talking about *Aunt Bina.*"

Is there somebody like "Aunt Bina" in your family?

Here are some other salable subjects my students came up with as they contemplated the uniqueness of their own family members:

"Turn Up the TV Set—Here Comes Grandma!" by a woman whose parents supplement their retirement income by acting in TV commercials.

"My Brother Is Different," by a girl whose brother is retarded.

"Wonder Woman Is Back—and She's Black!" by a woman whose sister is a high-achieving black woman.

"The Orneriest One of the Bunch," by a girl whose ninety-two-year-old grandmother used to sew the gold from her father's placer mine into her underskirts and transport it by stage from Elizabethtown to Springer, New Mexico.

"A Modern Miss with an Old Fashioned Talent," by a girl whose sixteen-year-old sister is a weaver and makes her own yarn from raw sheep-wool.

One way to get ideas for personality pieces is to brainstorm about what subject matter would be right for different sorts of publications. For the teen magazines, for instance, you would need teenage subjects with whom young readers could identify. Is there a teenager in your town who is achieving in some specific area? Sports? Art? Jewelry making? Is there one who has overcome a handicap to become an inspiration to others? What projects are local groups of teenagers undertaking? Are they into conservation? The restoration of an old church? Providing meals on wheels for the elderly?

Look at the special interest publications. Is there someone in your town who is accomplished at some specialized activity? Cross-country skiing? Rock collecting? Making patchwork quilts? One student of mine, Mary Hardman, sold an article to *Doll World* about an elderly lady who renovates old dolls and gives them at Christmas to the girls at a home for the retarded. How did Mary learn about this woman? Through her own retarded daughter, who was one of the girls at the home who received a doll. How did she learn about this specialty publication? She stood in front of a magazine rack and scrutinized its contents. *Doll World* was sitting there, waiting to be discovered.

What about the retirement publications? A number of them use material about senior citizens who are living interesting and worthwhile lives. Says an editor at *Mature Living*, "We are looking for articles about real people, not elderly saints. We want to know about vital older people who are doing interesting things and enjoying life to the fullest."

When I heard that, I submitted an article about my father.

Your local newspaper can be a source of subject material for personality pieces as well as for Drama in Real Life stories.

An example: I opened the paper one morning to read that the Great American Duck Race, held annually here in New Mexico, had just been won by an Albuquerque man named (you won't believe this) *Robert Duck*. Not only had one of Duck's ducks won the grand prize in this thrilling competition, but two of his other fowl had waddled off with second- and third-place ribbons.

When I phoned Mr. Duck to ask if he would grant me an interview, I found out that the whole Duck family participated in the training of the ducks. I learned also that Robert Duck had a delightful sense of humor and enjoyed making jokes about his unusual name.He not only gave me all the information I needed for a very funny story but also invited me over to take pictures of his ducks' backyard training area. The story was published in the *Woman's World* column called "Families."

Another example: My daughter Kerry ran across a small article in the paper about a mother and daughter who had started a home-based business called "Catered Calories." The two women, Norma Seebinger and Ginny Berger, prepared low-calorie meals and delivered them to people on diets. Kerry sold her article, "Diets To Go," to *Family Circle*, and Norma and Ginny were so delighted by the national publicity that they presented Kerry with some shares of stock in their business.

The Opinion Piece. This is exactly what it sounds like. You have a strong opinion about a controversial subject, and you support that opinion with personal anecdotes.

An example: In my early years as a mother, I wrote an opinion piece called "Let's Do Away with Togetherness." In it I presented the (then unconventional) theory that the family that does everything together was not necessarily happier and closer than the family in which members spent part of their time following individual pursuits.

When the article appeared in print, the number of letters that poured in from outraged readers was past anything I could have imagined. One woman suggested that I put our children up for adoption "so you don't have to do things with them." Another asked why my husband and I didn't move to Russia "where they don't have families." A third inquired as to whether we celebrated Christmas by shutting our children in the garage "with their own little tree so you won't have to watch their happy faces when they open their presents."

There were positive reactions too. One woman wrote, "Thank God for your article! It has saved my marriage. Last night I set up a card table in the den and served the kids dinner in there while my husband and I sat in the dining room and ate by candle light. We actually talked to each other during the meal! We are resolved that from now on we will do this at least once a week."

If you have ever felt neglected because your mailbox was empty, write an opinion piece and watch the mailman stagger beneath his load.

The How-To Article. Is there anything in the world you know how to do? If so, there are people waiting for you to share your knowledge. We are a nation of "do-it-yourselfers." Everybody wants to be able to do everything faster and better than everyone else, and nobody feels secure without advice from an expert. According to today's standards, an "expert" is anyone whose advice appears in print.

Chief among the markets for how-to's are the hobby and craft magazines. There are dozens of these, each catering to a particular interest.

Are you a talented amateur carpenter? Can you explain in a simple, step-by-step manner how you built an attractive rack to hold your wife's plants? How you constructed a miniature garage for your child's toy trucks? How you converted an extra bathroom into a home darkroom? Can you provide blueprints and photographs of similar projects advancing through their various stages of development? If so, there are magazines waiting to hear from you.

Can you design patterns for knitting, weaving, or embroidery? Are you into metalwork or making jewelry out of peach pits? Can you create your own lampshades, model ceramic vases, or come up with unusual and artistic holiday centerpieces: Is your Christmas tree different from everyone else's because of your homemade ornaments? Share your secrets and be paid for them.

Many of my students have hopped on the how-to bandwagon. Here are the subjects of some of their articles:

"How to Construct an Easy-to-Build Music Center"
"How to Survive in the Arizona Desert"
"How to Make an Earthworm Farm"
"Lost or Found? How to Teach Your Child Survival Skills"
"How to Make Your Own Stained-Glass Windows"
"How to Refinish Your Skis"
"How to Live with a Gifted Child"
"How to Live with the Ten Commandments"
"How to Sunbike in the City"
"How to Enjoy Sourdough Baking"
"How to Cross the Alps in a Hot-Air Balloon"

Here are some other possible how-to's for various publications:

For the youth magazines, tell teenagers how to be expert at tennis, save someone from drowning, make conversation, choose a college, write a love letter, get along with parents, recognize symptoms of venereal disease, take an exam, train a dog, survive their parents' divorce, decorate a dorm room, read palms, stop biting their nails, avoid getting pregnant, make a great pizza, find a summer job.

For the women's magazines, tell how to keep husbands, establish credit in your own name, lose weight, lessen housework, start a business, teach kids table manners, lay bricks for a patio, take good vacation pictures, raise herbs in a window pot, know if your children are on drugs, pack for a family camping trip, do tole painting, look younger, use up leftovers.

For the men's magazines, tell how to invest money, remodel the house, get rid of dandruff, buy insurance, get a raise, build a boat in the garage, burglarproof the home, keep a mistress, win custody of children, improve bowling scores, choose the right wine for company dinners, have a better sex life, climb a mountain, keep from having a heart attack.

How much do you need to know about a subject before you

start handing out advice? That depends upon the subject itself. Anyone who has ever taken a cross-country car trip with five children and a carsick dog is qualified to write an article on "How to Retain Your Sanity on a Family Vacation Trip." On the other hand, if your how-to is about something more technical, such as a piece for a craft magazine, you need to know the fine points of that craft. People who buy and read specialty publications usually have a pretty solid foundation of knowledge to begin with and are looking for advice and instruction from someone who knows even more. If your how-to piece contains medical or legal information, and you yourself are not a lawyer or a doctor, you will need to clear the piece with someone who is. Even if you are a victim of some dread disease and your article is based upon your own experiences, you cannot take it upon yourself to give medical advice to others.

These, then, are the types of articles that I have found to be the best vehicles for personal experiences. Having selected one in the light of what you have to offer from your own life material, you have one further decision to make before you settle down to the job of putting words on paper.

You need to decide which magazine you are going to write for.

> **. . . there are thousands of little-known people who are unique in their own ways and would be of interest to readers of specific publications . . .**

"What's in a name?"

Shakespeare would not have had to ask that question if he had known the Duck family of Albuquerque, New Mexico, who are exactly what they are quacked up to be—just *ducky!*

For four straight years, web-footed waddlers trained by Robert Duck and his wife, Kathy, have streaked to glory in the Great American Duck Race in Deming, New Mexico. The Ducks' dynamic ducks have thus far racked up winnings of over $9,000 for their delighted owners.

"That's before de-duck-tions," Robert hastens to point out.

The Ducks first learned about the race when they heard one

of its organizers being interviewed on the radio. Never one to duck a challenge, Robert phoned the station for more information.

"Because our name is 'Duck,' we'd always kept a couple of ducks as pets," he says. "We thought they might enjoy a trip to Deming."

That first year, there were 186 competitors in the race, and one of the Ducks' ducks came in third.

"That got us excited," says Kathy. "We thought, 'Why, we can really do this!' The next year we increased our duck team to 20 members and put them on a training program. Robert built a 25-foot racetrack in our backyard, and we made the ducks run it every evening."

The Ducks' ducks trained hard, and in the 1981 event, the speediest member of the team, B.F.D. (Bosque Farms Duck) Express, beat out 450 feathered competitors to win the blue ribbon. The press zeroed in on the event, and articles appeared in newspapers as far away as Cairo, Egypt.

The Ducks were joyous, but wary. Now they had a reputation to uphold.

"You've got to keep coming up with new ideas to give your birds the edge," says Robert. "We really quacked down on them and made them hustle."

Because the ducks seemed to be puffing up a bit, he and Kathy put them on a racing bird's diet of protein-rich grasshopper. They also designed a weight lifting program for them.

"We filled socks with sand and gravel and tied them to their ankles," says Robert. "The idea was that the ducks would pull the socks around while they ran after bugs, and that would strengthen their leg muscles. We had to discontinue this, though, because the socks kept getting snagged on bushes."

Even with this unpro-duck-tive setback, the Ducks' ducks were hot to trot when the 1982 race day arrived. There had been no re-duck-tion in the competition, but the Ducks had faith in their favorite, Quacky Simone.

"Be a winner—or be dinner," Robert whispered to her at the starting gate.

Adrenaline surged through Quacky at the horrible suggestion, and she tore down the track at tremendous speed, bursting across the finish line in a startling 1.406 seconds. The result was instant fame and an invitation from Johnny Carson to appear on the "Tonight Show."

After the show, which was a studio-shaking success ("Johnny and Quacky got along great," reports Robert), the Ducks, aglow with triumph, returned from Hollywood to begin preparation for the 1983 competition.

"We sensed this would be the big one," says Robert. "Thank goodness, our children were now old enough to work with us. They would give the signal—'On your mark—get set—go!' and Kathy and I would release the ducks onto the training track. This conditioned us all to react immediately to the 'Go!' command. With a race that lasts only seconds, release time can make a lot of difference."

The 1983 addition to the training program was a motorized treadmill.

"A friend who owns a laundry machine company donated a commercial dryer," says Robert. "At first it was too slick and the birds kept sliding around in it, but then we got the idea of smearing glue over the metal and throwing sand in to give them traction."

Though intriguing in concept, this new idea proved impractical.

"It made the ducks' toes sore," says Robert, "so, of course, we stopped using it. We wanted the thrill of victory, not the agony of D-feet."

The remainder of the training program was continued, however, and when trumpets in Deming again blared the Olympic anthem, Duck's ducks were prepared to duck straight into the chutes. The annual event had by this time become a grand holiday. There was a Duck Ball, a Duck Queen Contest, a Best Dressed Duck Contest, a Beautiful Duckling Contest for children, and a Hot Air Balloon Race.

Despite these frills, the main event was still the Duck Race itself. Uncounted multitudes of flapping contestants had entered the competition. There was even a Yuk Rent-A-Duck service for those who wanted to be part of things but had left their ducks at home.

The 1983 competition resulted in total triumph for the Duck family. First place winner was Duck Severinsen (named after Doc Severinsen, the band leader on the Johnny Carson show). Second, by a beak, came Ducky Letterman, and Lloyd the Duck—named after Robert's uncle—came in a respectable third.

The crowd went crazy! Confetti flew like feathers in a windstorm!

After gathering up their prize money, Robert and Kathy announced their plans to retire from competition.

"We've reached our 'beak!' " said Robert. "We've known true glory! It's not fair for us to keep accumulating honors. We don't want anyone ever to accuse us of fowl play."

The Ducks do plan to help officiate at future races, however, and they won't promise that they will never again compete. Robert, in fact, is already concocting a plan for future duck motivation if he and Kathy should decide to come out of retirement.

"We could feed the ducks green chili at the starting gate," he says, "and have ice cream waiting for them at the finish line."

("The Duck Bunch," *Woman's World*, 1984)

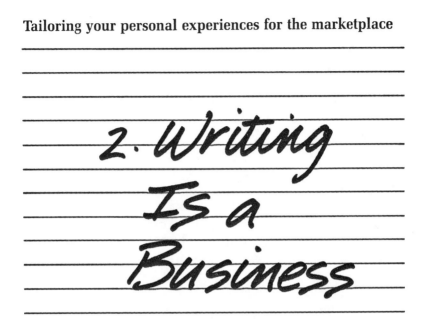

2. Writing Is a Business

If, as I have contended throughout the Introduction and the first chapter, "a professional writer is just an ordinary person," what is it, then, that makes it possible for him to sell his work? Why should he be receiving money for his personal experiences and enjoying the thrill of seeing them in print when other "ordinary people" have to be satisfied with recounting them in diaries and letters to friends?

What is the magic ingredient that separates the talented amateur writer from the no-more-talented professional?

In my opinion, it is one thing only—*attitude*.

The amateur looks upon his writing as an extension of himself, something created under divine inspiration, to be altered and tampered with by no one. If he feels that what he has written is good (and it very well may be, as there are some excellent amateur writers), he expects to be rewarded with a sale in much the way a child who has built a spice rack in shop expects to be rewarded by his mother with a hug and kiss. It makes no difference that Mom may already have a spice rack and not need another, or that she never cooks with spices, or that her spice containers are too big to fit the rack.

The child expects the gift to be evaluated in terms of the loving effort that went into it. If the reward is not forthcoming, he is shattered and reacts either with anger ("I made this perfect thing, and she's too stupid to appreciate it") or with crushed defeat ("I made the best thing I could, and since it isn't wanted, it must not be any good, and I'm probably not any good either").

The professional writer is able to be objective. He regards his writing as a business, and his stories and articles and books as products he is offering for sale. If his commodity is rejected, he does not consider it an insult. He realizes that he has probably offered the wrong thing to the wrong person at the wrong time, chalks it up as a learning experience, and sends his material somewhere else.

At the same time, he tries to figure out what *would* be right for the market that rejected him, so that next time he can offer something more in keeping with its needs.

An example to prove the point: Since the age of twenty when I gave birth to Robin, it was a dream of mine to sell a "Young Mother's Story" to *Redbook*. "Young Mother's Story," in case you are not familiar with it, is a monthly column written by *Redbook* readers who offer "practical and useful information" they would like to share with others on how they, as wives and mothers, are "dealing with the challenging problems of marriage and family life."

Well, *I* had problems. What twenty-year-old mother doesn't? So I wrote them down and submitted them, and promptly got them back again with a printed rejection slip.

During the next year new "problems of marriage and family life" cropped up, so I tried again. Another rejection.

At twenty-two, I had another baby, and sibling rivalry reared its ugly head. I was almost glad to see it, as it gave me another subject to write about. I submitted a new article. I received a new rejection.

By now I was getting thoroughly irritated. Here were all these little nobodies who had never written anything more than high school essays getting $750 apiece for their rambling accounts of breast-feeding and toilet training, while I, who had been writing for magazines for years, couldn't crack the market! It was humiliating.

So I tried again. And again. And again. Every year, as regular as clockwork, I wrote a new "Young Mother's Story," and every year, just as regularly, it was rejected.

Finally the day came when I knew the article I had written was the best I was capable of producing. I called it "Whatever Happened to Childhood?" and it dealt with Don's and my struggle to keep our thirteen-year-old daughter Kerry out of the dating game for another year or so. It was a subject about which I had strong feelings.

"I love my children," I wrote in my final paragraph. "We all love our children. But might it be that with this very love—with our gift to them of so much so early—we are in reality depriving them of the greatest gift of all?"

It was a tearjerker. Absolutely beautiful. I was certain that the editors of *Redbook* would not be able to resist it, and I was almost right. They held it seven months. When they returned it at last, it was accompanied by the following letter from the articles editor:

> *Every now and then it is my unpleasant duty to reject a story which strikes me as well written, timely, and meaningful. In the case of your story "Whatever Happened to Childhood?" several other members of the staff share my opinion, if that makes you feel any better. In considering stories for our Young Mother's series, however, there are several ironclad rules we must follow. One of them is that the writer's children cannot be older than eight or nine. It is because of this rule that we are rejecting your story.*
>
> *In closing, let me suggest that you submit this story to some other women's magazines—Good Housekeeping, McCall's, etc.*

It was a gentle way of putting it, but I got the message. What this editor was trying to tell me, ever so nicely, was that I was no longer *a young mother!* I, who still got carded when I ordered wine in a restaurant, was too decrepit for *Redbook* readers to find anything in common with! I staggered under that blow for weeks.

If I had used my common sense, though, I would have realized from the beginning that this particular article was not *Redbook* material. *Redbook* is a magazine that caters to a readership of educated women between the ages of eighteen and thirty-two. A little elementary math would have told me that if a woman graduates from college at twenty-two, marries immediately and has her first child a year later, by the time she reaches the upper edge of the *Redbook* reader's age level, that child will be no older than nine.

Every magazine has its ground rules. With *Redbook*, the emphasis is on age. With *Good Housekeeping* the demand is for stories with conservative values and upbeat endings. (They turned down one of my stories because my heroine had a hysterectomy, which the editors felt was too depressing a subject for their readers to tolerate, especially in fiction.) *Michigan Out-Of-Doors* wants "personal adventure and ordeal pieces—very unusual incidents encountered while hunting, fishing, and camping." *Guideposts* also uses "ordeal pieces," but only when the ordeal was survived with God's help.

No matter how fine your writing itself may be, you cannot write a story for one of these publications and expect it to be right for the others. You cannot fit a square peg into a round hole. The story about your abortion will not go to *Good Housekeeping*. The account of how you skipped church on Sunday in order to go forth into the wilderness to slaughter a grizzly will not go to *Guideposts*. *Redbook* will have no interest in an article on how your faith in God helped you adjust to life in an old folks home.

I eventually sold "Whatever Happened to Childhood?" to a magazine called *The Woman*. I also, twenty years after my first hopeful submission, managed to sell *Redbook* a "Young Mother's Story." The story that finally made the grade was called "Our Daughter's Double-Diet Problem" and was about Kate, a victim of celiac disease, which is an extreme allergy to foods that contain a protein called gluten. Kate was two when the disease was detected and four at the time the article was written. I was careful not to refer to the ages of my other children.

The biggest problem with this piece occurred when *Redbook* requested a picture of Kate and me to run with the article. I hate to recall how much film we used before Don was able to get a shot that was blurred enough to disguise the silver-flecked hair and crow's feet which become the lot of one who is no longer a "young mother."

How do we learn about these all-important ground rules? There are several ways, one of which is to subscribe to writers' magazines which have marketing columns. There are two of these which are particularly helpful: *Writer's Digest* and *The Writer*. These are published monthly and are available through subscription as well as on many newsstands. Another valuable source of marketing information is the *Writer's Market*, a large, hardcover book published annually by Writer's Digest Books. This contains the names, addresses, editorial needs and taboos of literally thousands of outlets for freelance material. *Writer's Market* can be purchased at most bookstores, and if it is not in stock it can be ordered. It can also be consulted in the reference sections of most public libraries.

But the best way of all to find out about magazines is to read them. Stand at your friendly neighborhood magazine rack and thumb through them, not as a prospective reader looking for entertainment, but as a business person casing the markets for a product he has for sale. Try to zero in on the special feel of each publication, and ask yourself who the typical reader might be.

Start with the cover. This has been carefully designed to catch the potential reader's interest. What do you find there? Is it a famous figure? What sort—a political personality, movie actress, or skateboard champion? Is it a professional model? If so, what image is he or she presenting? This will give you a clue as to the image the editors feel their readers will best relate to.

Is there, perhaps, a child on the cover? If there is, what is it doing? Does its activity tie in with an article in this issue of the magazine? Is it wearing a cap or sweater that readers can knit themselves by following instructions provided within?

Is the cover a scenic? If so, what emotion does it evoke? Serenity or excitement? Does the scene tie in with a travel article? You will find that the articles the editors think will hold most attraction for their readers are listed on the front cover. What are they? Knowing this will steer you in the right direction when it comes to proposing article ideas of your own.

Now open the magazine and run your fingers over the paper. Is it shiny and slick with a high gloss or pulpy, like the paper on which newspapers and comic books are printed? You will generally find that magazines that can afford the cost of good paper will also be able to afford to pay decent fees to their contributors. The slick paper will reproduce color, which means that the magazine can run high cost color advertisements. These bring more money into its till and, you can hope, into yours as well.

And about those advertisements—what are they for? You can learn a lot about the typical reader by analyzing the products he or she is being offered.

The managing editor of *Ms.* once described to me that magazine's effort to establish its tone.

"In the very early issues we consciously set out to acquire advertisers whose products are not connected stereotypically to women's lives," she said. "We put in tremendous effort for several years to attract advertisers of such things as cars, stereos, corporate and life insurance. We wanted to make the point to our readers that we were a magazine that believed that women have the same adult interests that men do. When we felt we had created the environment of a realistic product universe for our readers, then and only then did we begin to run ads for cosmetics and other personal products. We wanted them to fit into our pages in the same proportion that they do into the lives of our readers."

Once you have studied what a magazine is selling, it is time to determine what it is buying. Notice how many articles it uses each issue, on what subjects and with what slant.

Does it use fiction? If so, how much and of what sort? Is the fiction tightly plotted or open-end slice of life? Is it serious or humorous? Romantic or mysterious? About how many words do the stories run? Are they written in first or third person? Is the protagonist usually male or female?

You will be surprised at the things you can discover. I make this sort of perusal every month, varying the newsstands, and I have never yet come home without a new market to aim for. New magazines crop up every day, and old ones fall by the wayside. The birth of each new publishing venture provides a new opportunity for writers.

What can you offer all these magazines? The chances are there are people and events in your life that will be of interest to many of them. What about a personality piece? *Working Woman* has a column called "Career Options" about women who have created unusual careers for themselves. Do you know such a woman? Several of the teen publications run thumbnail sketches of achieving teenagers. Is there one in your neighborhood? Is there an animal in your life who is particularly clever or has done some amusing things? Three of the confession magazines pay good money for short features about their readers' pets. Let Fido pay for his own dog food by becoming a story subject. One confession magazine buys original prayers. Another pays for "true psychic experiences." Can you open your heart and share with others those words with God that have helped you most? Can you write an account of a "psychic experience" that shocked or startled you?

What about the juvenile magazines? Surely there is something in your life that you can offer those. If you have children yourself, you know their interests and capabilities. Choose a subject about which you are knowledgeable and explain it to a child in words he can understand. What about a how-to? Children are always interested in learning how to do things. Tell them in simple, step-by-step terms how to build or make something.

Do you hold a job? If so, you have a ready-made subject to explain to others. Let the real-estate salesman from Ohio come forth with an article for one of the publications aimed at young marrieds, cautioning them about the ripoffs to avoid when going forth to purchase their first home. Are you a teacher? Tell the readers of one of the parents' magazines how they can help their problem reader develop a love for books. Are you a garage mechanic? Tell us, please, what to look for when we go out to buy a used car! Tell it to the readers of men's magazines. To the readers of teen publications. Tell it to *Single Parent!* (How many women must there be who are for the first time in their lives faced with making such a purchase on their own?)

All of us have lives that are rich with article material. The question we must ask ourselves is, "Who is the particular reader to whom this material would be interesting, and which magazines does he buy?"

Sometimes a subject will appeal to many types of people. In that case, you have a choice as to how to approach it. In recent months, for instance, I have seen a number of different articles about a training school for clowns in Venice, Florida, only a few miles from my native Sarasota. *Seventeen* ran a personal experience piece by a teenage girl who was one of the students in this special school, while *Modern Maturity* ran a photo story featuring the elderly clowns who volunteer to teach their profession to the youngsters who will one day take their places. There was an article in an in-flight publication (one of those giveaway magazines you find on airplanes) describing the clown school as "an interesting place to visit when you are traveling through Florida," and another in a children's magazine called "How Would You Like to Be a Clown?"

This business of making your subject fit a special market is known as "slanting," and it is one of the most important parts of writing as a professional. If your personal experience does not sell to the magazine for which you originally intended it, you will often need to readjust it to fit another. Sometimes these revisions will have to be made a number of times before the story finds a home.

Gil Johnson, a student of mine at the University of New

Mexico, had an article idea so unique that I was certain from the moment he discussed it with me that he would place it. The question was, where? Gil had started the first class in the country in karate for the blind. Under his tutorage, students became so adept at judging speed and direction of attack by the sound waves bouncing off wall and floor that they were able to compete against opponents who were fully sighted.

What magazine might be interested in such a subject? Gil's first thought was that it might be right for a First Person Article for *Reader's Digest*. The *Digest* runs a series of such pieces—dramatic, humorous, or inspirational—for which they pay $3,000. Because of this high pay, competition is terrific, and the editors can afford to be highly selective. Gil's story was rejected.

Gil consulted *Writer's Market* and decided that his next submission would be to *Guideposts*, an inspirational, interdenominational publication, edited at that time by Norman Vincent Peale. This submission meant making some cuts in the article. The story as Gil had originally written it ran 2,500 words: *Guideposts* articles run a maximum of 1,500.

The article was rejected by *Guideposts*. Why? Because it was written in the first person from the viewpoint of Gil, who was the class instructor. *Guideposts* uses first-person stories, but wants them to be from the viewpoint of the person who has "overcome obstacles, risen above failures, met sorrow, learned to conquer himself, and become more effective through the direct application of the religious principles by which he lives." The editor suggested to Gil that he might want to rewrite the story as an "as-told-to" piece by one of the blind students. Gil decided this would be a last resort if he could not sell the story under his own name.

Gil again rewrote the article, slanting it this time toward *Black Belt*, a martial-arts publication. For this magazine he expanded the article to 4,000 words and emphasized the techniques he had used in teaching karate to blind teenagers.

Black Belt took the article, which was published under the title "They Conquered the Night." They also took Gil. The boy was snatched right out of my hands and hauled out to

California to become *Black Belt*'s assistant editor.

The job offer came so fast, and Gil's move was so sudden, that he never had the opportunity to take the photographs with which to illustrate his story. Once in Los Angeles, he wrote asking if I would try to get some for him. I rounded up the youngsters, and Don and I spent an interesting afternoon snapping pictures in our basement rec room as the students went through their routines. During that time, I became enchanted by the only girl in the group, a pert, eighteen-year-old college freshman named Debbie Gonzales. Blind since birth, Debbie had joined the karate class because "I always like to try something new."

I queried *American Girl*, asking if they would be interested in a piece about Debbie. They were, from the angle of how a bright, energetic teenage girl managed to live a full and normal life despite a visual handicap. The story, "Debbie Gonzales Can Take Care of Herself," was published with photographs. It was later reprinted in a fifth-grade textbook published by Scott, Foresman and in a book called *Vistas* published by Houghton Mifflin.

This, then, is "slanting." It is simply the process of analyzing markets and writing a story in such a way that it meets their requirements.

Objectivity about one's writing is a difficult thing for most people to attain. This is particularly true for those of us who utilize our personal experiences. In offering others portions of our own lives, we are, in a way, offering portions of ourselves. It is difficult indeed not to take the rejection of our stories as a rejection of us, as people. After the initial shock of having a manuscript returned, there is a great temptation to tuck it safely away in a drawer so as not to subject ourselves to further hurt.

But the writer who wants to become professional cannot afford to protect himself in this manner. He must rally and send his story off again. Gil, with his karate piece, could have been so crushed by his first two rejections that he might never have sent his story to another market. If that had been the case, he would have missed not only a sale but a career in publishing.

Objectivity about their work may come more easily to men than to women, for men are generally more used to competition. For those of us who are housewives, almost everything we do is for those who are near and dear. Our payment for services rendered is affection and appreciation. If we cook a meal and set it on the table and nobody eats it, we feel that we have failed, not just as cooks, but as wives and mothers.

"If they loved me," we tell ourselves, "they would have eaten it no matter what it tasted like. They would care more about my feelings than about their stomachs."

By the same token, when I get all dressed up for a party, I expect my husband to tell me that I am beautiful. It is beside the point that I am not. The effort I have taken in primping and perfuming must be acknowledged. I do not want to be looked at objectively, but through the eyes of love.

Life in the business world is not like that. Editors are not going to buy a story from you just to make you happy. They won't buy it because you need the money to pay a dental bill. They won't buy it because you stayed up till 3:00 a.m. writing it and then had to get up at 6:00 a.m. to go to work. They won't buy it because you are a nice, deserving person who needs a little sunshine in your life.

There is only one reason why an editor will pay you good money for an article. It is because it is right for the magazine and for the people who read it.

If you wish your story to be read by people other than your loved ones, you will have to make it right for its market.

. . . twenty years after my first hopeful submission, I managed to sell *Redbook* a "Young Mother's Story" . . .

When I was a little girl I was pudgy. I suffered the agonies of having to wear chubby-size dresses, being the last chosen for relay races and receiving humorously insulting valentines while others got ones with hearts and lace. My first adolescent crush drove me to a crash diet that slimmed me down to proper proportions, which with effort I have managed to retain. But I never forgot the miseries of my grade-school days, and I was determined that when I had children of my own, they would never go through the same experience.

From the beginning, I planned to instill good eating habits, serve nutritious, well-balanced meals and control between-meal snacking. But as every mother knows, the best parents are those who have not yet had children. Fate has a way of defeating our best intentions. My plan worked well enough with our first four children; but Kate, our fifth, was different.

This difference was not immediately discernible. For the first six months of her life Kate seemed like all the rest of our children—plump, healthy, energetic and exceptionally good-natured. She took a regular bottled formula with no problems, started on the routine baby foods in the usual order—fruit, rice cereal, vegetables and meats—and delighted in everything.

The first inkling of trouble seemed so minor we hardly noticed it. I went away on a short trip, and when I returned, a couple of things had happened—my oldest daughter had done the grocery shopping and Kate had mild diarrhea. She also had a slight cold, so I assumed the diarrhea was caused by the mucus she was swallowing. I never thought about the fact that on her shopping trip my daughter had purchased mixed cereal for Kate instead of the usual rice cereal.

Almost immediately after my return home, my husband and I began to prepare for a vacation trip. The first day on the road, Kate began to vomit. The vomiting continued throughout the week. We could not wait to get home to our pediatritian.

When medication and bland diet had no effect on Kate's condition, our doctor began a series of tests that went on for months. One by one she eliminated such terrors as cystic fibrosis, stomach ulcers and intestinal tumors. While these tests were going on we struggled valiantly to get some nourishment into our baby . . .

("Our Daughter's Double-Diet Problem," Redbook)

3. The Research Called Living

It may seem strange to think in terms of "researching" an article based on personal experience. It will seem less so, however, if we define "research" as the collecting of data, the gathering of material. We do such research every day of our lives. It may be done at a coffee klatch where we hear about the problems of finding a decent rest home from a neighbor who is searching for one for an aged mother-in-law. It may be done at a PTA meeting where we listen to teachers and parents hashing over the results of a new type of grading system. It may be done at the corner grocery store where the manager pauses to answer our questions about the reason for a sudden rise in the price of cheese.

We may do research on the golf course, in the emergency room of the hospital, at the office water cooler, or at a junior high track meet. Wherever there are people willing to share themselves with us, there is research to be done.

It may not be immediately apparent how such research can best be put to use. We simply know that what we are hearing strikes a chord. We find it interesting, and therefore assume that it will be interesting to others. We file it away in our minds, or jot it down in a notebook, and let it germinate. In some cases, this may be the end of it. In others, it will develop slowly in the subconscious, and we will wake one morning thinking, "Hey, there's a story here!"

The story may be one we can sit down and write immediately, or it may require some further preparation. Sometimes this will include a trip to the library to consult the *Reader's Guide to Periodical Literature.*

With the exception of the word processor, the *Reader's Guide* may be the nonfiction writer's best friend. Published annually since 1905 by H. W. Wilson Company, this set of books lists by both author and subject matter all the material that has been printed in leading American magazines since the year 1900.

The *Reader's Guide* can be useful in two ways. To begin with, you can take an article idea to the *Guide* and see which, if any, magazines have published articles on the same subject in recent years. This will save the time and effort of sending a story to a publication that has covered the subject in a previous issue.

Second, and perhaps even more important, you can research a subject by looking up the title, volume number, page, and date of publication of each magazine that contains relevant material. The library should have not only the bound editions of the *Guide* from earlier years, but also paperbound, semi-monthly supplements on currently published material. Once you know which issues of which publications you need, you can tell the librarian, and she will either steer you to them or go back into the depths of the library's private heart and dig them out for you.

I have found the *Reader's Guide* invaluable and have practically worn a path through the library floor from the front door to the desk where it sits.

On one occasion, for instance, I received an assignment from a women's magazine to write a personal experience article on the subject "Face-Lifts That Flop." I myself had never had a face-lift, but I had a neighbor, Connie, who'd had one and was terribly upset over the result. The problem was, she didn't know how to tell me about it. All she could do was wail pathetically, "Isn't it terrible! Don't I look just sickening!"

Well, she did have some scars, and one eyelid drooped a bit, but then, I knew nothing about plastic surgery. Maybe that's how people were *supposed* to look one month afterward.

I had a lot of questions. What actually does a face-lift consist of? How do surgeons cut and pull and trim and sew a sagging face in an attempt to make it young and beautiful? Is there more than one kind of face-lift? How long should an operation of this kind take? What should it cost? How much pain is natural afterward? Is it always done in a hospital? How long is it before the bandages come off? What should the patient look like immediately after? How long is it before she starts looking good?

It was obvious Connie was in no state to give me factual answers. I needed background knowledge before I could begin to tell her story.

I went to the library, turned Kate and Donnie loose in the children's room, and headed for the *Reader's Guide*. There, under "surgery, plastic," I found listed every article on face-lifts that had appeared in the top national magazines. The librarian helped me locate the issues; I photocopied the articles, collected the children, and went home to study. When I was finished, I had enough basic knowledge to ask intelligent questions ("Was your operation a simple meloplasty, or did it include a blepharoplasty?") and enough case histories to compare with Connie's so that I could appreciate how her condition differed from the norm.

I wrote the article.

Connie sued her doctor.

Another example is the story of Ellen, whose husband beat her black and blue at least once a week. After putting up with this treatment for twelve years, she discovered Women's Haven, an underground refuge for battered wives. Ellen packed up her two children, moved into the haven, and after three weeks of "getting her head together" in a supportive atmosphere, gained the strength to get a divorce and build a new life for herself and the kids.

It was a great story. Hooray for Ellen! But there were some things she could not tell me. Was Women's Haven unique, or were there other such shelters scattered about the country? If there were, where were they? How were they financed? How did desperate women gain entrance? How many passed through their doors each year?

In the *Reader's Guide* I found reference to a study supplying just this information and was able to expand upon Ellen's personal story to give the article broader scope.

The *Guide* is just one of the resources the library has to offer. Many libraries offer guided tours to acquaint people with their reference materials. If yours does not, ask the librarian to take you around and point things out. Librarians may not know everything, but they do know where to go to look everything up, and I have yet to meet one who wasn't friendly, helpful, and delighted to be of assistance with writing projects.

If you have small children, a good time to visit the library is during the story hour which most libraries sponsor for tots. Stick the little ones in the children's room to be entertained and race for the research area. Everyone will be happy.

There is another sort of research you will be conducting as a writer of personal experience articles, and this is the live interview. To some people interviewing comes easily; for others the process is more difficult to master. I fall into this latter category. Because I am shy by nature, my first attempt at conducting an interview was a disaster.

The assignment was to fly to California to do an interview for the "Can This Marriage Be Saved?" series in *Ladies' Home Journal*. I was to talk to husband, wife, and marriage counselor and write the story of the once-threatened-but-now-salvaged marriage in first person from all three of their viewpoints.

This was the first assignment I had ever been offered that entailed travel. It was also the first assignment I had ever received from the *Journal*. The editor who had written me to "try us again in ten years" had long since left the staff, and I had been trying for *thirty* years to break into this market. I wasn't about to turn down this opportunity. Still, the idea of grilling strangers about something as personal as their marital problems made me terribly uneasy.

"Please, let the issue be a simple one," I prayed as I got off the plane at the Los Angeles airport. "Let it be nosy in-laws, misbehaving children, a lack of communication—anything, as long as it doesn't involve intimate revelations."

Obviously, the Lord thought I needed toughening up. The couple's problems turned out to stem from the fact that for five years the wife had been sleeping with her half-brother. The interview took four hours, delayed as it was by floods of tears from the wife and roars of outrage from the husband. By the time the ordeal was over, the couple, the counselor, and I were emotional wrecks.

In the cab on my way back to the airport, I decided to play back the interview on my tape recorder to see if it was as dreadful as I was afraid it was. To my horror, I discovered that in my nervousness I had neglected to press the "record" button down hard enough. The tape was blank.

Although I shudder to recall that interview, it was a learning experience. Since then I have written more than two dozen articles for that series, and I know a lot more about how to do an interview.

I have even reached a point at which I feel qualified to offer a few suggestions:

1. When you are going to interview somebody, make an appointment and arrive on time. Your subject is doing you a favor by letting you barge into his life. Don't inconvenience him by making him wait or by taking up more time than the interview has been scheduled to cover.

2. Do your homework ahead of time. Find out enough about the subject so that you can appreciate what he has to tell you.

I was commissioned once by *New Mexico Magazine* to write an article titled "How Our Land Feels to Us" about six of our regional woman artists. I know as little about art as anyone could whose whole artistic background has been admiring kindergarten artwork taped to the refrigerator door. When I received the assignment, I went to the galleries where the artists were exhibiting their work so that I could get some idea of their styles and techniques. I looked up biographical material, collected their brochures, and read other articles that had been written about them.

By the time I faced my subjects, note pad in hand, I was able to ask questions that, while certainly not those that would have been asked by another professional artist, were intelligent enough for a layman. The women invited me to join them on a sketching trip, and I was able to watch firsthand the methods each used and how each treated the same subject differently. It was a fascinating experience, and one I could not have appreciated if I had not obtained basic information about the artists to start with. I did not have to spend our valuable time together asking such things as, "In which galleries is your work displayed? What prizes have you won? Who did you study under?"

A surprising bonus came from that assignment. When the article was published, the artists were so pleased that each gave me a miniature painting as a thank-you present. I was overwhelmed. Since I had been paid for writing the article, I felt *I* should have been thanking *them*.

3. Remember that it is the subject, not you, who is the important person during an interview. We are all so used to the give and take of social conversation that it is hard sometimes not to want to take our own share of the limelight. If the subject describes an interesting experience he has had, your immediate impulse might be to counteract with a similar experience of your own.

Control yourself. Sit on that impulse. Ask a question instead, and listen to the answer.

4. Don't be afraid to let a silence fall.

Here again, it is a matter of conditioning: most of us equate silence with boredom. The moment voices stop we rush in to fill the gap with sound.

But the subject has been conditioned that way too, so let him take over the job of gap filling. Often you will find that you get your best material this way. You ask your question and the subject answers. A silence falls. You don't do anything about it, so the subject feels compelled to. So he starts speaking again, and offers something more, often an anecdote to illustrate a point he has been trying to make, or a colorful comment, or a personal observation. The interview may suddenly switch direction as a whole new area of interest opens up before the two of you. If the subject is carrying the ball and the new direction appears to be an interesting one, follow him. Don't try to shut him up so you can get on to your next prepared question. There will be time for that later. For the moment, ride with the tide. You may end up with something very special in the way of a story.

5. Notice more about your subject than what he says. While you are looking at him and listening to him speak, think in terms of adjectives and adverbs. What are the details that will bring him alive for others?

The subjects of my *New Mexico Magazine* article were all women and all artists, and they all painted the same general subject matter. On careful observation, though, they were extremely different. The colors and the techniques they used reflected their personalities. So did the atmosphere in which they chose to work. One painted in seclusion, while another had her easel set up in the family rec room. One chose to portray skies heavy with storm clouds, while another made them clear and blue. One worked slowly, devoting months to each painting. Another kept several paintings in various stages of production at all times, moving from one to another so that she never had to wait for paint to dry. Observing these things provided an insight into the women, not only as artists, but also as people.

6. Try to frame your questions so that they will not be answered with a flat "yes" or "no" or with dead-end statements.

I recall with embarrassment an interview I did in my earlier years. It could and should have produced a wonderful article. Our daughter Kerry had come home from a junior high track meet to announce that the winner of the high jump competition had one arm and one leg.

Kerry tends toward exaggeration, and I suspected that the boy might be missing a finger or toe. Still, I decided to investigate. I attended the next meet, and yes, this kid was just as Kerry had described. He approached the bar on his one strong leg with great, kangaroolike leaps and jumped 5′ 8″ to take the city championship.

I phoned the boy's family and asked if I could interview their son, and they agreed. I blew it. The moment I entered their home, I froze. I simply couldn't think of a thing to say. I was so afraid of treading on tender ground that I didn't tread *anywhere*. In my worst nightmares I still hear myself saying inanely to the boy's mother, "You must be very proud of your son's accomplishments," and hear her reply, "Yes, I am."

If I were conducting that interview today, I would know enough to handle it differently.

"How did you feel when you first realized that you had borne a child with such a handicap?" I would ask her. "Were the doctors able to give you any idea of what might have caused it? What were the most significant problems you had to face as your boy grew? Which of his accomplishments make you most proud? Why? How did you manage to do such an extraordinary job of raising him to fulfill his potential as a human being? Did you receive any counseling? What advice can you give other parents who might be faced with such a challenge?"

But the opportunity is gone. I never sold the article.

One of the best interviewers I know is Joe Bell, whose Drama in Real Life articles appear regularly in top national magazines. Joe's skill in relating to people makes him the recipient of assignments that would finish me off completely.

"The toughest I was ever faced with," he says, "was a piece I did for *Good Housekeeping* about a family whose children were afflicted with a rare disease and were dropping off one by one. The parents wanted research done and felt that by publicizing the situation they might find help for the children who hadn't yet been stricken.

"Every minute of that one was painful, but what really hurt was that *Good Housekeeping* didn't run it right away. When they finally scheduled the story, they asked me to go back and find out if the girl who had been critically ill when I did the original interviews had died. I drove around the block a lot of times before I rang their bell, and it was only because we had established a good and firm relationship that I was able to do it at all."

Joe feels the interviewer must establish rapport with the interviewee within the first few moments they are together.

"If you don't do this quickly," he says, "it may not occur at all. You have to care about the person you are talking with: if you don't have curiosity and concern, you're in the wrong business. These are the greatest assets in interviewing just as they are in carrying on an animated conversation at a dinner party. Use reasonably good taste in what you ask, but don't be afraid to ask pointed questions. Otherwise the interview becomes a waste of time."

How do you take down information during an interview? There are several possible methods, and pros and cons of using each. Despite my traumatic experience with the incest story, I have continued to use a tape recorder, although I now take written notes for back-up. There are writers who disagree with this practice, feeling that the presence of the recorder causes subjects to freeze. They also point out that listening back over an entire interview of taped material is extremely time consuming.

My own experience has been different. I've found few people self-conscious enough to be intimidated by the recorder. There may, at times, be a little initial stiffness, but before many minutes have passed, the subject becomes so engrossed in the details of his story that the instrument seems to fade into the woodwork. Admittedly, transcribing the tapes can be a chore, but in the process of listening and typing, I often discover nuggets of valuable material that I somehow managed to miss when it was originally presented. I find it much easier to bring life to a subject's experiences if I can refer not just to jotted notes but, also, to the phrasing and inflections of a voice.

There will be times when you as a writer will find yourself in need of information from someone who is not available to be interviewed in person. In this case there are two alternatives: the letter and the telephone. When you write to a subject for information, it is smart as well as courteous to enclose a stamped self-addressed envelope. Most people are stirred to action by the sight of an envelope with a stamp already on it: they feel compelled either to steam off the stamp or to put something in the envelope and mail it, and the latter course of action is much the easier. In fact, if you want to be absolutely certain of receiving a reply, use a special-delivery stamp. It will cost you something, true, but it takes a person of iron willpower to drop such an envelope into the wastebasket.

Interviewing by phone presents some problems. You may not be able to get through to the subject, or you may hit at an inconvenient time. He may be irritated by your intrusion into his privacy and refuse to talk with you. He may not have information available to give, and won't have had time to look it up.

Still, it is surprising what some people manage to accomplish with telephone interviews. A student of mine named Joanne—a bright, outgoing, warm-hearted individual who loved the whole world and took it for granted the feeling was reciprocated—used to amaze the class by coming up with incredible quotes from the most astonishing people merely by phoning them. She phoned everybody—state senators, governors, movie stars, television personalities, newspaper editors, doctors, lawyers, psychiatrists, and on one occasion, the wife of the President of the United States—and projected such magnetic exuberance that such people chatted with her at length.

I have often wondered about the size of her phone bill, but Joanne certainly did come up with some colorful stories.

Arnold Hano, author of some 500 magazine articles for both adult and juvenile publications, once remarked, "Even in my earliest years as a beginning writer, I never had any trouble getting interviews with well-known celebrities. The thing that has surprised me all my writing life is that people in general are more willing to do favors than not."

As I have said before, library research and interviews are vital in particular instances. But the primary source of research for the personal experience writer is day-to-day living. We research what it is like to have a baby through natural childbirth, to see a child through a near-fatal asthma attack, to cook tasty meals on a budget, to keep a teenager from going the drug route, to learn to get along with in-laws, to be fired from a job in midlife and have to make a new start, to adjust to the death of a parent, to build a marriage that will hold up under a multitude of stresses.

"Research" is another word for learning.

Using that research by putting it on paper in a form to be shared by others is creative writing.

. . . The subjects of my *New Mexico Magazine* article were all women and all artists, and they all painted the same general subject matter. On careful observation, though, they were extremely different . . .

They appear to be a half dozen housewives on a picnic. In jeans and windbreakers, they jam a station wagon crammed with cameras, sketch pads and peanut butter sandwiches. They're not picnicking, though. They're off to work.

These six New Mexico artists will sketch all day in a rock-walled canyon north of Santa Fe, yet the paintings to emerge from this expedition will be so varied that you will see little relationship between them.

They seem to have little in common except that all live in Albuquerque. They come from across the country. There is a 30-year span between the oldest and the youngest. Jean Parrish paints slowly and singlemindedly in a quiet studio facing the west slopes of the Sandia Mountains, while Betty Sabo works in a freeway for pets and teenagers. Carol McIlroy's impressionistic oils are aglow with golds and oranges; Pat Harrison prefers watercolors, her colors subtle, skillfully blended. Jane Mabry's pastel portraits depict Indian dignity and humor. Egg tempera gives Doris Steider's detailed landscapes a luster that is almost ethereal.

Still, there is a common denominator. These women paint New Mexico in all her moods, her canyons and skies, her mountains and forests, her villages and peoples. The flushed walls on an adobe church at sunset. Dark trees, heavy with snow, bent low over a frozen stream. The same trees in fall, alive with color. An Indian fiesta. The blaze of chili peppers against a frame doorway. The fields of spring, flat and green against a high, rich curve of sky.

"We want to catch it before it's gone," says Betty Sabo, speaking for all of them. "This land ... how it looks ... how it feels. How *we* feel about it. Things are changing so fast. The world is sweeping in on us. We want to leave some record so that when the Southwest as we know it is gone, people will be able to remember ..."

("How Our Land Feels to Us." *New Mexico Magazine*)

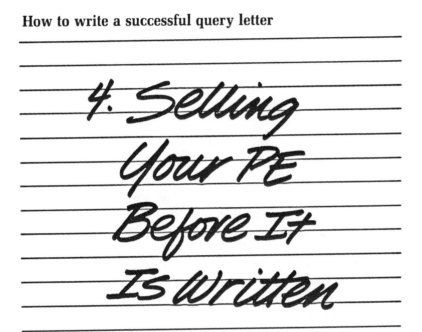

4. Selling
Your PE
Before It
Is Written

In this book I am going to discuss the ways in which personal experiences can be utilized in both articles and fiction. Each type of writing has its merits. In one way fiction may be the easiest area in which the straw-into-gold writer can work because it generally requires little outside research. Fiction comes straight out of your head. You can write an entire novel without ever leaving the house.

But article writing has one thing going for it that fiction does not. It is possible to sell an article before it is ever written. The way you go about this is to write a query. A query letter is a letter of proposition. You write to the editor of the magazine and offer him your article idea. Is he interested in it or isn't he? If he is, you write the story. If he is not, you don't. Or you query somebody else.

A query letter is not a condensation of an article, nor is it an outline. It is more like a job application. It should be short, usually no more than one page, and in it you want to do the following things:

Introduce yourself. By this, I don't mean you start off by saying, "Hello there. My name is Peter Jones." (This may sound ridiculous, but you would be amazed at how many beginning writers do exactly that.) You are going to sign your name at the end of the letter anyway, so you don't need to waste space by giving it twice. What you do want to do is to introduce yourself as a writer who is offering an article idea for consideration, and to let the editor know briefly why you are qualified to write the piece.

If you have writing credits to offer, here is the place to mention them: "I am a freelance writer whose work appears regularly in *Esquire, Playboy,* etc." If you are a beginning writer with no published work behind you, you may still have strong qualifications because of your knowledge of the subject matter. One student of mine, proposing an article on "Beating the Insurance Racket," had had personal experience working as a claims adjuster for six major insurance companies. Another, writing about "How to Handle Your Money When Traveling Abroad," was a retired banker.

Or you may have qualifications that are less technical and more personal:

> As a divorcee with three children, I would like to propose an article about the social problems a woman faces when she is single and a mother. With a foot in each camp, she neither fits into the world of married couples, nor has much in common with the swinging singles group. Having lived with this situation for two years, I have found a way to . . .

One word of caution. Remember always that a query letter is at heart a sales letter. With it you are trying to sell the editor on the fact that the story you propose is right for his particular magazine and that you are the one who ought to write it. Don't say anything that is going to work *against* you. Never be negative—"I'm not a professional writer, and I'm not sure how to go about this, but I thought I'd approach you on it anyway, just in case you might want to give a beginner a chance." That might get you Brownie points for honesty, but it is not going to get you a go-ahead to write an article.

State your article idea in a nutshell. A magazine editor is a busy person. He may read dozens of query letters a day, as well as an equal number of finished manuscripts. He does not want to have to work his way through paragraph after rambling paragraph while he tries to figure out what it is you are actually suggesting. Lay it right on the line, in one sentence if possible: "I would like to write an article for you about my daughter's success in overcoming physical and emotional problems following a craniotomy." If your article is totally out—perhaps he has recently purchased a personal experience piece about brain surgery—he can stop reading right there and send you a note saying, "No, thank you."

Elaborate briefly. Explain to the editor how you plan to develop your idea. One of my students wrote about a teaching program for gifted children. In her query she gave a one-sentence description of the program, a sample anecdote about a child who built a huge set of plastic teeth to demonstrate the need for good dental care, some statistics about the number of youngsters who participated in last year's program, and some quotes from the teacher who had originated the program and the principal of the school that used it.

In this portion of your query, you can demonstrate your writing style and show the editor that your article will be lively, interesting, and fun to read. If you are a budding Erma Bombeck, this is the opportunity to let it be known.

Let the editor know that you are familiar with his publication and are planning to gear the article to his particular readers.
Here are queries that brought go-aheads to some of my students:

To *Seventeen:*
I am a 19-year-old college student who, during the past year, had the opportunity to study and travel through Latin America. Seeing quite a variety of handicrafts and fearing that I would be returning to an empty bank account. I had an idea: Why not let travel pay for itself by arranging to ship back to the United States and sell there some of these products?

After arousing the interest of some friends in selling my goods, checking with U.S. customs, and learning about import regulations, I began my business and the hole in my bank account was slowly refilled.

It would seem to me that *Seventeen* readers, who are at the age where you dream of travel and wonder how to get the funds to go about it, might be interested in an article suggesting a way in which they can make their dreams reality.

If this idea appeals to you, I could base an article on my own experiences. Readers would be one step ahead of me because in my case all was learned by trial and error.

I hope you will consider this article proposal, and give me the opportunity to pass on the good word that wealth is not a requisite for the young traveler.

Sincerely,

Patricia Doherty

Here is one that got a go-ahead from *Home Life:*

I recently had an experience that rekindled my faith in God and totally changed my life. I am interested in sharing it with the readers of your magazine.

I am a senior at the University of New Mexico. Last month, as I was driving with friends through the beautiful mountains east of Albuquerque, we chanced upon a sign indicating that we were close to Camp Inlow, a Southern Baptist youth retreat. I was a camper at Inlow several summers as a young girl, and had not been there since I was 12. We drove to the camp at my insistence and walked around for perhaps an hour. As I walked through this peaceful place and recalled so many happy times I'd had there, I began to feel again the nearness to God that I'd experienced as a child.

The article I propose to write would relate this experience and my subsequent rededication to Christian living.

So many young people today, when they leave home to attend college, begin to gradually leave behind the church and its values. I had done this. My experience last month proved to me that childhood teachings in a Christian home where God is a meaningful presence are never really lost. I think my story might serve to illustrate to your readers the importance of Christian retreats for children.

I look forward to hearing from you.

Sincerely,

Nancy Gore

Let's take a look at exactly what these girls have done:

Patty has no writing credits with which to introduce herself, but for *Seventeen* magazine these are not important. Her age is. *Seventeen* buys a lot of material from teenagers, and the fact that Patty is under twenty is a strong selling point. After introducing herself, Patty presents her article idea concisely, and it is a good one. She does not take a broad, overall topic such as "What It's Like to Spend a Year of Study and Travel in South America," which could well be nothing more than a teenager's diary, but narrows down her experiences to a single angle—how she made the adventure pay for itself. She then tells the editor why *Seventeen* readers—not just any readers, but these particular ones—would be interested in this subject.

Nancy's letter is more subjective. Using her common sense, she has addressed her proposal to a Baptist publication. (She certainly would not have been able to sell an article on the value of Baptist retreats to a Catholic or Jewish magazine.) She is able to state her theme in a nutshell. "The article I propose to write would relate this experience and my subsequent rededication to Christian living."

In her final paragraph, Nancy explains why she believes her article would be of special interest to *Home Life* readers. At the end, she tacks on the practical suggestion that the story would illustrate the significance of Christian retreats for children. This is a good selling point. Religious retreats must be funded, and a sincere testimonial by a college student who has benefited from having attended one might well inspire donations by wealthy church members who have before this not realized their importance.

Here is a query to *Mature Living* that brought a go-ahead to one of my older students:

What is the most important legacy a person can leave future generations? His memories.

What is the most appreciated gift a mature person can present to his friends and relatives? A written record of the most interesting events of his life.

I am 64 years old and have recently been a teacher of eighteen senior citizens. They wrote short sketches of their most moving memories and called them their "personal myths." Their memories of long-past incidents, character studies of parents and other relatives, diaries, letters, and family stories handed down over many generations were the raw materials of their writings. Several said to me that they didn't want to be just names and dates on a family tree. They wanted to be known as the persons they were; they wanted those who come after them to know what they were like and how they felt about the unique events which shaped their lives.

How to write such material effectively, how to make inexpensive "books" for preservation and for gifts, and encouragement to do so, would be the content of an article that I would like to write for your magazine.

Would you be interested?

Sincerely,

Carlton W. King

Carl has used a question-answer approach in hooking the interest of an editor. He then identifies himself as being the right age to relate easily to readers of a retirement publication. He shows empathy for this specialized group of readers and offers them a product they can afford on their limited incomes.

Mature Living is a Baptist publication. Inspired by his success there, Carl eventually wrote a different article on the same subject and sold it to a Methodist retirement magazine.

Here is a query that brought a go-ahead from *Christian Single:*

I would like to write an article for *Christian Single Magazine* about my experiences with the difficulties and rewards of beginning a college education at the age of 31, after the breakup of a long marriage. Since so many women are returning to college and careers these days after many years as housewives and mothers, I feel that an article on this subject would be of interest to your readers.

I intend to focus on the personal alienation I felt beginning freshman classes with students more my daughter's age than my own, and the challenge of learning to discipline myself to study again and juggle classes, work, motherhood, and coping with the emotional pain of my pending divorce. I feel that this story might inspire other women to have the courage to continue their education and build a future for themselves in the new role of head-of-the-family and only breadwinner.

The rewards of making the decision to become a college student in my 30's have far outweighed the difficulties. I am now a senior at the University of New Mexico, majoring in advertising, and will graduate from the university at the same time my daughter graduates from high school.

Would you be interested in such an article?

Sincerely yours,

Susan Minser

Susan's short, punchy letter does the job. In only a few paragraphs she manages to give a clear idea of what the article will be like. She emphasizes the fact that there will be an upbeat ending with a nice twist—mother and daughter graduating together—and states why she feels her experiences will be inspiring to the readers of this particular magazine.

To *Homeowners How To Handbook:*

I am a student who recently transferred from the Northeast to a southwestern university. The 2,000-mile move and reestablishment in a new apartment presented me with a number of problems, the two most immediate being a lack of furniture and a limited budget. I also knew that there was a good chance that I wouldn't be staying long in the first place I found, and a second or third move would only be complicated by the bulky used furniture that I was able to afford.

My solution was to build inexpensive but attractive furniture, based on my own designs, with the few tools that I had brought with me—furniture that can be "knocked down" in minutes, moved with ease, and reassembled just as easily in a new house or apartment.

I would like to share with your readers my designs for a matching couch and coffee table that I have built with the ideas of simplicity, economy, and appearance in mind. Both pieces were designed around the butcher-block motif, require only hand tools to build, and involve less than $75 in materials. A beginner can easily build either, and a more experienced craftsman would be justifiably proud of the results.

I would be happy to provide photographs and detailed blueprints to cover every phase of construction.
Yours sincerely,
Erik Schichtel

Since what one person considers "attractive furniture" might not seem that to someone else, Erik enclosed a photo of the pieces.

What sort of response can you expect from a query letter?

A cautious one, usually. An editor can tell you that an article idea seems appropriate for his publication and that the subject has not already been assigned to somebody else. He may offer you some helpful hints about what approach to take and what length to make the article. What he probably will not do is tell you, "Great! I'll buy it sight unseen." Until you have written for a publication often enough so that the editor is familiar with your work, he had no way of knowing if you can deliver an article as promised. The world is full of "idea people" who cannot sit down and put enough words on paper to make up a full-length article. Usually an editor will ask a new writer to submit a finished story "on speculation," which means that he is interested and will give the manuscript a careful reading, but he retains the option to reject it if it is not as good as he hoped it would be.

In other words, a go-ahead is not the same thing as an acceptance.

There was a time in my teaching when I did not make this distinction clear enough.

A student of mine, Bob Turner, submitted a query to *Home Life* about his relationship with his father who was fifty-two when Bob was born. *Home Life* likes stories about family situations, and the fact that Bob was a Baptist and black didn't hurt matters any. The editor responded that the article idea sounded interesting and he would be happy to review the completed manuscript "on spec."

Bob went off like a skyrocket. He phoned me at home and

read me the letter. Then he took it to class and read it there. The next thing I knew, he had phoned his parents in the little town in Texas where they lived and told them the good news that he was making his father famous. Bob's mother was so excited that she rushed down to the church and informed the pastor, who announced from the pulpit the fact that "our own Mr. Turner is being honored by *Home Life* magazine." The congregation burst into cheers, and plans were made for a "Mr. Turner Day" on which the article would be read aloud as part of the Sunday sermon. A collection was taken up to import Bob himself for the grand occasion.

By this time I was out of my mind, racing down the halls of the journalism building (have you ever tried to catch up with a quarterback in a hurry?) crying, "Wait, Bob! Wait! You haven't even started to write the article yet! How do you know the editor is really going to buy it?"

"Of course he'll buy it," Bob said with certainty. "He says right here in his letter that the idea 'sounds interesting.' "

By the end of the semester, Bob did finally get around to sitting down at the typewriter, and *Home Life* did accept the article. It was published in a Father's Day edition, and I assume "Mr. Turner Day" went off as planned. But I still have nightmares about what would have happened if the story had been rejected.

... An editor may offer you some helpful hints about what approach to take ...

Dear Lois:

I'm delighted to have you working on another assignment for *Woman's Day.* This is to confirm our telephone discussion of the article on "How to Solve Sticky Money Problems."

The piece needs authority, of course, but you do not have to quote an expert in answering each question or group of questions. You might just announce in the introduction that you've discussed the problems with experts in various fields, but some of the best solutions came from ordinary people who learned them from trial and error.

I think it's also wise to admit—in the introduction or elsewhere—that while most sticky situations can be resolved satisfactorily, not all can. Sometimes we are caught between a rock and a hard place and are forced to make a choice. Is the money important enough to risk losing a friend? Or is the friendship so treasured that you are willing to put up with an annoying habit (such as failure to repay loans) in order to preserve it?

One problem you might want to use is that of splitting checks in a restaurant. Many people are annoyed by the person who orders extra courses or the most expensive dish on the menu and then says, "Let's divide this in half," yet no one likes to appear cheap or to be one of those equally annoying people who quibble over every quarter.

Keep in mind that we're looking for a lively article with lots of tips and suggestions. We're not interested in long psychological analyses of why people behave the way they do.

I hope this is all clear. If you have any questions, don't hesitate to call me collect. We are prepared to pay you $3,000 for this. Can you deliver the ms by the end of the month?

Best regards,
Rebecca Greer, Articles Editor

5. The Foolproof Recipe

The preliminaries are over. You've chosen an experience to write about, one that is meaningful to you and will be (you hope) to others. You've decided on the form you will use for your article—personality piece, how-to, or drama-in-real-life. You have selected an appropriate magazine and queried the editor, and he has answered, "That sounds possible. We'd like to see it on spec."

So, what do you do now?

No, you don't go rushing for the typewriter, not quite yet; you don't take off on a cross-country trip without a road map. First you make very certain you know where it is you are heading, and then you figure out the best way to get there.

There is a formula that is generally used for article writing. If this sounds intimidating, we can define "formula" as "an established way of doing something," a way that has prov[en] so consistently effective that people continue to use it [over] and again. There is no rule that says they have to do t[hat;] just do it because it works. Most of us understa[nd in]-stinctively. We use formulas for measuring an[d] shelves, preparing seedbeds in a garden, cutting and sewing dress patterns, and baking cakes. There is no law that says that we have to mix ingredients into a cake batter in precise amounts and in a certain order, but if we don't the cake doesn't rise and nobody wants to eat it.

The same holds true for writing most magazine articles. There is a general pattern of construction that is used consistently because the articles that result from it seem to turn out well. There is no law that says this pattern must be used, but your chances for a sale will be greatly increased if it is.

This is how an editor of *Empire Magazine* describes his concept of good article construction:

"I think of an article as having four general parts. The writer needs to organize his research so that his outline conforms to them.

"First, there is the lead, which is what gets your reader to start reading. Then there is a statement of theme in which the writer states what it is he intends to tell people. Then comes the body of the article, which is the actual meat and bones and flesh. And, finally, there is a conclusion at which point the writer tells people what it is he has told them and rounds it off with something that leaves them feeling good about the whole reading experience. In my years as an editor, I have rejected more articles for organizational faults than for any other reason."

Translating this into my own terms, here is the recipe:

Take one hook (any type you choose).
Follow with a directive statement.
If there is potential opposition, anticipate it.
⸻⸻⸻⸻⸻ of the article by alternating different
⸻⸻⸻⸻⸻ ιch a way as to keep the reader interest-

⸻redients one by one and see how they

The Hook. You can call this the lead or simply the beginning. I prefer the term hook because that is what you want your first few paragraphs to be, a hook that snags the reader and won't let him go until he has read through the entire article.

The "hooking" has to be done quickly. Open any magazine, and one glance will show you why. The average article starts about halfway down the page, perhaps sharing space with an illustration. After a couple of paragraphs, you will find in italics a statement that the story is continued on page something-else. At this point, the reader has a decision to make. Is he going to turn to page something-else, or isn't he? Once he decides instead to flip over the page he's on and see what the next story is about, you've lost him. He may intend to come back to your article later, but chances are he won't.

Probably the most commonly used hook is the anecdote, a little story with characterization, color, and action. When used as a hook, it leads into the directive statement.

Here is the anecdote I used as a hook for "Ten Sticky Money Problems and How to Solve Them":

> When I was in third grade, a girl named Olivia borrowed money from me to buy a Coke. She never paid me back.
>
> I was too embarrassed to ask her for the money. I didn't want her to think I didn't trust her.
>
> One day, I went to school to find Olivia absent. Permanently. She had moved with her parents to Philadelphia, and my money had gone with her. I was outraged!
>
> Even today, all these many years later, I still am outraged! I wake in the night with Olivia's throat in my hands! Surpassing my fury, however, is my contempt for my 8-year-old self for not having stood up to that pigtailed shyster and demanded what was mine.

Another kind of hook is the "startle statement." You make an announcement that shocks the reader and jerks him upright in his chair, gasping, "That can't be true!"
An example:

The day I died, it was raining.

This is the first line of a story by a student who had been pronounced dead from drowning and then, amazingly, was revived.

A third sort of hook is the "poetic prose lead" that catches and holds the reader because of its sheer beauty. Needless to say, the subject of the article has to be sufficiently poetic itself so that the hook isn't just tacked on to the front of the article, as out of keeping as a velvet evening gown on a tennis court. You wouldn't use a poetic prose lead on an article about how to clean fish.

An example:

> A Florida spring is strange. It does not explode upon one in the way that a northern spring does with bare branches bursting out suddenly in leaves and grass leaping greenly through darkened puddles of melting snow. A southern spring comes softly, for there is no great contrast. It is a softening of the air, a lifting of the heart.
>
> It was in just such a spring that I first began to notice the scabby-kneed, flat chested little girl who had lived next door for eighteen years—had grown up.

This is the lead for an article by a student who married his childhood playmate.

No matter which type of lead you choose, remember that it has to serve two purposes; it should grab and hold the reader's interest, and it should set the scene for what comes next—the directive statement.

The Directive Statement tells the reader what the article is going to be about.

Here is my directive statement for the money problems article:

> It would be nice if I could say that the experience with Olivia taught me a lesson. Regrettably, that is not the case. The

sad truth is that, as a long-time adult, I still have problems
with situations involving friendships and money, and many
of my friends tell me they do also. The stickiest situations
seem to be those in which the amounts at stake are comparatively small ones and it hardly seems worth the risk of alienat-
ing a friend in order to collect them. At the same time, we resent the fact that we are being treated unfairly, and our buried
hostility threatens the very friendship we are struggling to
preserve.

Here is the directive statement from Gil's *Black Belt* article:

> This blind man is one of a small, experimental group of ka-
> rate students who have learned both to handle an assailant on
> the street and to "see" with mental sight in perfect blackness.
> They are the only karate class of blind people in existence. I
> am their instructor.

There it all is in a nutshell. The reader now knows the direction the article is going to take, and he can choose whether
or not he wants to go along. The directive statement is important to the writer as well. By composing it, he gets it clear in
his own head what his goal is and exactly what he is setting
out to say.

It is amazing how many beginners, especially when they
are writing personal experience articles, set out to put words
on paper without having the faintest idea where it is they are
heading. They just take a general subject, sit down at the
typewriter, and pour out everything they can find to say. The
result all too often is a motley, disorganized mess.
An example:

My student, Paul, had spent the previous summer as a fire
fighter in a national park in Colorado. The experience had
been the high point of his life, and he wanted to share it with
the world. Paul's article was twenty-eight pages long. In it he
told about his trip to Colorado (it was the first time he had ever been on a train), the scenery, and the pretty girl who was

his seat companion. He described the park itself, the rushing rivers, the mountains, the crows that flew in for just one day and then flew out again, the other fire fighters (one of whom was an Indian with an "inscrutable face"), the food they ate, and each one of each day's activities. He told about the training they received, the equipment they used, and the time they thought there was a fire but there really wasn't. He told about being homesick, about the bears that got into his food supply, and about gaining ten pounds during the course of the summer.

It was the sort of epistle every mother would love to receive from a son who was away for three months. It was *not* a magazine article.

"What is your directive statement?" I asked Paul. "Can you put into one paragraph or, better, into one sentence what it is you are trying to prove with this material?"

He regarded me blankly. "I'm saying what it was like up there."

I tried to rephrase the question. "What conclusion are you building to? What is the point of it all?"

He shrugged.

I made some suggestions.

Did he want to make this a personality piece about the Indian? For that his hook could be a poetic prose description of the man's craggy face as seen in the flickering light of a campfire. The directive statement might be something to the effect that, "Little did I guess when I met this strange and silent man that he would teach me a whole new value system." The body of the article could then be a study of his relationship with the Indian.

Or what about a how-to on fire fighting? The hook could be an anecdote about a fire in past years that did terrible damage. The directive statement: "Today, because of scientific advances, we have equipment that can keep this from happening." The body could contain descriptions of this new equipment and the techniques that are making forest fires easier to control.

Or his story could be inspirational. His hook could be a description of himself, scrawny, insecure, leaning out the train window for one last glimpse of his mama's face as he pulled out of the station in Albuquerque en route to a he-man summer in Colorado. The directive statement: "Could I possibly survive this challenge?" The body of the article would then utilize the material that showed Paul's personal growth during his fire-fighting summer.

"But if I wrote the story one of those ways, I'd have to leave out some of the stuff," Paul objected. "Like if I wrote a profile of the Indian, I couldn't tell about the cute chick on the train."

"Right," I said. He was catching on! "But if you wrote the inspirational article, you could include her. You could show how she snubbed you on the trip up, and then demonstrate how miraculously the summer changed you by having girls fall all over you on the trip back."

Paul frowned. "But then I'd have to take out the stuff about the crows. I liked the crows."

"No matter which way you go, you're going to have to dump the crows," I told him. "And a lot else too. No magazine editor is going to even consider printing a story as long as yours. You're going to have to cut it at least by half."

Paul stalked out of the classroom in fury. The next day he dropped the class. I was sorry, because he really did have good material for not only one article but several.

Anticipation of opposition is not necessary for every article, only for those that are in some way controversial. The more controversial your stand, the more important it is to acknowledge your awareness of the fact that there are people who hold opposing views. By doing this, you keep your article from sounding totally one-sided, and yourself from sounding self-righteous and narrow-minded. Having acknowledged your opponent's position, you proceed to refute it and to convince your readers that it is invalid.

When my student, Steve, wrote his article about his May-December marriage, he realized that there would be some readers who would react with horror to the thought of a match between a man of twenty-six and a woman of fifty. To ignore this fact would be to leave the article incomplete.

Steve anticipated the opposition by presenting the arguments against such a marriage at the beginning of his article:

> This alternative to the more conventional marriage style has not in the past met with social approval. While, I'm sure, other men have seen the beauty and strength of "older women," there has, at least until recently, been a kind of unspoken taboo connected with them. Such a relationship would seem to strike a blow to one's masculinity (he's probably not virile enough to satisfy a younger woman), or to smack of some unresolved Oedipus complex.
>
> But none of this was on my mind that warm Saturday afternoon four years ago at La Jolla beach when I looked up and saw. . . .

And then, having conceded that negative views could exist, Steve continued on to prove with his true-life experience that, in his case at least, they were not valid and that his marriage was a union of two happy, well-matched individuals who simply chose to ignore the difference in their ages because of all the other, more important things they had in common.

This is where I made my mistake when I wrote "Let's Do Away with Togetherness," the article I cited earlier in this book as an example of the personal opinion piece. I pushed my controversial views so hard without giving the other side of the question recognition that I antagonized my readers.

The body of the article takes up the largest number of pages and follows the path laid out for it by the directive statement, building point by point toward the **conclusion.** The rather simplistic conclusion I was seeking to reach with my money problems article (let's face it, the issue at stake was not one of world-shattering importance) was that, sticky as they were, the problems could be solved.

I wound up my story by touching base again with my anecdotal hook:

If I were to run into Olivia today (those graying pigtails wouldn't fool me for a minute; her image is indelibly engraved on my memory), I like to think that I would have the strength of character to step right up and say, "Olivia, I have an overwhelming desire for a can of soda pop. How about coming up with the cash I loaned you forty years ago?"

If she did, indeed, hand it over, I think I might be able to forgive her and renew our friendship—despite the fact that, today, you can't buy a Coke with a dime.

Some editors expect writers to submit their article proposals in detailed outline form before they will consider offering them an assignment. Even in those cases when an outline is not requested, it is hard for me to imagine any writer being able to successfully construct an article without one.

This is an article outline that got me a go-ahead from *Dynamic Years*, the official publication of the American Association of Retired Persons. This magazine is tailored for people in the forty-five to sixty-five age range.

ARTICLE PROPOSAL: PARENTS COME LATELY
(THE PROS AND CONS OF LATE-IN-LIFE PARENTHOOD)

Hook:

Like most working housewives whose time is tightly scheduled, I keep a list of **Chores for the Day** taped to the refrigerator door. Last night an old high school classmate stopped by after dinner to discuss plans for flying home together for our thirty-fifth class reunion. She took one look at my list and burst out laughing.

"I can't believe this!" she exclaimed. "Right after your reminder to yourself to **Make Plane Reservations,** you've got a note saying **Find a Substitute to Drive Kate's Carpool.** I'd forgotten what it was like to plan your life that way. That's the sort of note I find on my *kids'* refrigerators!"

Directive Statement:

Her reaction didn't surprise me; it's one I've grown used to. For most of our friends whose own children flew the coop a good ten years ago, it does seem strange to see a pair of their contemporaries driving carpools, chaperoning middle school field trips, and supervising Girl Scout cookie sales. For my husband Don and me, however, this is our life. Although we're in our early fifties and have three grown children (one of whom will soon be making us grandparents) we are still up to our ears in the strenuous and often exhausting parenting of a teenage son and daughter.

Body:

According to Shakespeare's list of life stages in his comedy *As You Like It*, the average person's lifetime ideally should be divided into units which coincide with chronological age. If that held true for us, in the words of the Bard, Don would have "eyes severe and beard of formal cut," and I would be "full of wise saws and modern instances." As things currently stand, however, Don owes the shadow on his chin to the fact that his razor was borrowed by our son to clip the dog, and the wisest of my "wise saws" consists of the oft repeated statement, "If you don't turn down that stereo, you're going to go stone deaf!"

Historically speaking, there's nothing new about delaying parenthood. Back before the Industrial Revolution, late marriages were prevalent in Europe where a couple had to prove they had the property and means to support themselves before starting out on their own. Late parenthood followed that ruling automatically.

Today it seems that we may have come full cycle. Recent studies document the fact that in the United States over the past three decades there has been a steadily increasing trend toward older parenthood.

Reasons for increase in older parenthood:

1. The increasingly high cost of child rearing. Children are no longer the economic asset they were when most families lived on farms or ran small businesses. They have become a luxury item, and people postpone having them

until they can afford them. (Will get quote from someone who has done this.)

2. Good jobs require more years of training than they used to, and both men and women stay in school longer and therefore postpone both marriage and parenthood. (Will get statement from bigwig at large university as to average age of student today compared to twenty years ago.)

3. Advanced methods of contraception have made child postponement easier, and advances in genetics and obstetrics have removed most of the hazards of bearing children beyond the optimal reproductive age.

4. The increasing divorce rate. Four out of five divorced people remarry, and many of these middle-age unions lead to second families. (Personal experience interjection; this was the case for Don and me. Another example would be our next door neighbors, Bob, fifty-six, and Peggy, thirty-eight, who are the parents of a six-year-old son and a two-year-old daughter.)

Detriments to late-in-life parenthood:

1. Having gray in your hair and wearing bifocals. Kids are by nature conformists; they are easily embarrassed by anything that makes them stand out from their peers. (For parents this may turn out to be a blessing in disguise. The knowledge that the mothers of Kate's classmates tend to be ten to fifteen years my junior provides strong motivation to keep struggling against middle-age spread.)

2. Having less physical energy with which to deal with the challenges of parenthood. I intend to interview a high school or Little League coach about what differences he may have found between the involvement of older and younger parents in their children's athletic activities. (Quote from Bob Turner, a former student of mine who was born when his father was fifty: "My dad wasn't into playing catch or shooting baskets with my kid brother and me like the fathers of a lot of our friends. We always knew, though, that when game time came, whether it was foot-

ball, basketball or baseball, he'd be up there in the stands cheering his lungs out.")

3. The fact that the society today's kids are growing up in is very different from the one we older parents knew as children. Younger parents are more in tune with contemporary issues and so may be more easily able to contend with the problems of today's youth. (Don and I were prepared to deal with a teenager who swigged beer at a party, but we were stunned when we discovered that our son was smoking pot. Don admits too that he feels ridiculous initiating a father-son discussion about the facts of life with a kid who for the past three years has been subscribing to *Playboy*.)

4. Lack of freedom to enjoy the footloose middle years. (Friends invited Don and me to join them on a cruise of the Caribbean. We would have loved to go, but there was no way we were going to leave town when our scatterbrained son had just gotten his driver's license.)

5. The fact that children of older parents may not have the chance to know their grandparents. (On Grandparents Day at Kate's school, she was the only one in her class with no guest to bring.)

Benefits of late-in-life parenthood:

1. Parents' careers are likely to be well established. They are better off financially and able to afford a more comfortable life-style. They are also more likely to be in a position to hire household help and babysitters.

2. Since financial pressure has been cited by marriage counselors as the #1 cause of dissension in marriage, middle-aged couples who have fewer money problems often have more stable, happier relationships. Children benefit from this emotional security.

3. Because they are more mature, older couples tend to be less self-centered and more responsible than younger ones. (A study conducted by Corrine Nydegger of the Institute of Human Development at the University of Cali-

fornia at Berkeley showed that older fathers felt less strain and discomfort in their roles than fathers in their twenties, and that men who became fathers during their mid-thirties and forties found the adjustment much easier than younger fathers.)

4. Having young children tends to keep parents thinking and feeling younger than their years. (President Jimmy Carter, who was forty when his daughter Amy was born, stated, "She makes me feel young again.")

5. Couples who wait for parenthood may appreciate it more and get more enjoyment from their children. (Will support this statement with a quote from such a parent.)

Conclusion:

There are midnights when I'm lying awake, waiting anxiously for Donnie's souped-up hot rod to pull into the driveway below the bedroom window, and I think, "Other women my age are peacefully asleep right now."

There are times when I'm walking through the supermarket, wheeling a grocery cart filled with the ingredients for twenty-one gigantic meals plus a ton of snack food, and I think, "Other women my age go out to dinner a lot."

There are times when the house is shaking with the blare of conflicting stereos, one blasting disco and one hard rock, and I think, "Other women my age are sitting in quiet houses, relishing their solitude and reading Judith Krantz."

When I have those thoughts, I admit I feel a bit put upon.

But there are other times too—last night, for example, when we were sitting at the dinner table, and Donnie was telling "Knock, knock" jokes, and Kate was doing her imitation of Michael Jackson, and suddenly the dog came running into the room with its hair styled in a purple Mohawk.

We all started laughing, and Don turned to me and said, "You know, hon, this is just about as good as it gets."

"Yes," I said, "it probably is."

And I meant it.

Windup:

So, while it may be true that "All the world's a stage, and one man in his time plays many parts," it is also true that for some crazy people, the role of parent seems to fit quite nicely and naturally into Act Three.

(completed article appeared in *Dynamic Years*)

6. Polishing Your PE

When I was in my middle thirties, Tony Hillerman, then the head of the journalism department at the University of New Mexico, asked me to become a part-time faculty member and teach a class in writing for magazines. To say I was surprised is an understatement. Not only had I no teaching experience, my marriage at an early age had prevented me from going to college.

That unwise and unsuccessful first marriage lasted nine years. In the time that followed, I learned how to write as a professional. A divorcee with three small children to support, I was not able to sit around waiting for inspiration to strike or to be precious about my work. I wrote every day, and I wrote to sell. By the time I met and married Don four years later, I had learned a lot about magazine writing. It was for this practical knowledge, certainly not for any academic qualifications, that I was hired at U.N.M.

I faced the first day of class with more terror than any eighteen-year-old. Don had encouraged me to accept the position, but now, suddenly, I was struck with the realization that my students, all upperclassmen, would be far more educated than I was. I had never taken a course in writing; I had simply *written*. How did people go about teaching others to write? What, in fact, was a college course supposed to be like?

I finally decided to design a course that would resemble as closely as possible the situation my students would encounter when they left the university and set out to make a living in the outside world.

When the first set of assignments was turned in, I wrote critical comments and handed them back for the first rewrite.

"Rewrite!" a wide-eyed coed gasped in bewilderment. "But you haven't even graded them!"

"How can I grade them?" I asked, equally bewildered. "You haven't finished writing them."

"Mine is finished," she snorted, glancing about at her classmates for support. "A paper doesn't have to be perfect to get a passing grade."

I drew myself up into what I hoped was a professorial stance and delivered my first lecture:

"There is no such thing as a B or a C in Magazine Writing. Your article is either salable or it isn't."

I mellowed a bit after that first traumatic semester. I did grow to accept the fact that in college there are B and C students whose major interest is in some field other than writing, and I began to grade for effort and attitude as well as for production. I eventually came to accept papers that came in past deadlines (though I took off points for them), and to take a sloppy first draft from a beginning typist. I even adjusted to the inevitability that no matter with what dignity I began the term as "Ms. Duncan," I was going to finish it as "Lois."

The issue on which I did not give in was the rewrite. That was too important. My students wrote their articles, and wrote them a second time, and a third, and more if necessary, until both they and I considered them salable. Then, like releasing birds for flight, we sent them into the market.

And in many cases, they flew!

Over the eleven years I taught that class, my students sold to such varied publications as *Holiday, Saga, Home Life, Mature Living, Highlights for Children, Good Housekeeping,* the Denver Free Press, Catholic Digest, American Girl, New Mexico Magazine, Young Miss, Country Gentleman, Seventeen, Woman's World, Cosmopolitan, Outdoor Arizona, Ceramics Monthly, Southwestern Sports, Living With Teenagers, Rolling Stone, Empire, Black Belt and a number of others.

What exactly is a rewrite, and why is it so important?

To begin with, I think it is necessary to rewrite in order to allow the first draft to be spontaneous. Writing habits vary from person to person, but my own technique is to follow my general outline and pound out the first draft at top speed without giving a thought to detail. Like an athlete approaching a high jump, I have no time to think about being beautiful; I am trying to pick up enough speed to sail over the bar. If I stop to worry about whether my position is graceful or who may be watching from the stands or whether my hair is staying in place, I, like the high jumper, will never get my feet off the ground.

My first drafts are very rough. I wouldn't want anybody to read one. If, when I die, there should be a first draft lying on my desk (and there probably will be, because there always is), I want it to be burned. All I hope to do with a first draft is to give my story shape and movement. I find this especially necessary when writing at length. With a novel, it's easy to find yourself with a string of compartmentlike chapters, each an entity in itself, instead of one great sweeping whole. By keeping a fast pace without pausing to search for the perfect way of saying things, I find I am better able to achieve a sense of continuity.

There are, of course, successful writers who do not work this way. There are some, I've heard—I can't say that I've ever actually met one—who write with such precision that their original wording cannot be improved upon. Their first copies are their final ones; no rewrites are necessary. Such writers do exist, but I cannot believe that there are many.

In one of my recent classes, there was one particular student who was both the bane and the delight of my existence. He was bright, funny, talented, and so prolific that stories of all types—mysteries, juveniles, romances, psychological thrillers—rolled out of his typewriter at the rate of several per week. Then he put them into envelopes and sent them away.

"Here's a copy of my new story," he would say, handing me a carbon. "I wrote it yesterday."

"Where is the original?" I would ask him, already sure of the answer.

"On its way to *Playboy*." Then, seeing my expression, he would smile ingratiatingly. "I know you want us to rewrite, but I just don't like to work that way. When I've finished something, I'm through with it. I want to get started on something else."

Which is understandable. But, did it work? Did his stories sell? No, they didn't, and they should have. For he had talent and sensitivity and drive—all the elements necessary for a successful professional. But he was releasing his birds with their wings still imperfect, with their tails trailing in long drooping arches behind them and their feathers of uneven lengths. He would not admit that this was the reason they didn't reach the treetops.

"It's the editors," he'd mutter. "They don't even look at the work of newcomers. They have their stable of regulars, and they won't buy from anybody else."

But these regulars were once newcomers. People are breaking into magazines every day.

People like Eva.

Eva Schoonover was my mother-in-law's best friend. Mom and Eva lived next door to each other on the rural outskirts of the little farm town of Morenci, Michigan.

One day Eva wrote a story. She called it "Mr. Big." It was about an experience from her past that held great meaning for her, and she wanted to share it. She typed it up, mailed it off to a magazine, and it was rejected. Eva felt terrible.

My mother-in-law, who had an awesome amount of faith in me, consoled her.

"Now, don't worry," she said. "Don and his family are coming for a visit next week. You give Lois your story and she'll fix it up and sell it for you."

When Mom told me this, I almost died. I *love* Eva! I couldn't bear to hurt her feelings. Yet how could a woman with an eighth-grade education, with no writing background, have, out of the blue like this, produced a story that somebody would want to buy?

Well, I learned my lesson. The story was beautiful. The only problem was that Eva had taken it through one draft and no further. I spent perhaps a total of twenty minutes helping her with polishing. We mailed it off, and Eva's check came back by return mail.

Eva's story is short, and so, with her permission, I am going to use both versions of it to show the difference a small amount of polishing can make. Here's the first draft—as it was when she first showed it to me:

Mr. Big
by Eva Schoonover

It was a beautiful May day, after a very cold and wet spring, when my husband announced we would plant the garden.

Doug, our 7-year-old grandson, was spending the week with us. He had muscular dystrophy and was having trouble walking. He lived in the city so planting a garden sounded exciting to him as well as to our son, Dan, age 10.

Dan loved watermelons so he grabbed a package of watermelon seeds, while Doug was fascinated by the pumpkin seeds we had saved from their Halloween pumpkin. I tried to explain to him that since this was a small garden anything with vines was out. No more was said, but I saw tears in Doug's eyes.

Both the boys helped us until Doug got tired and had to stop. We helped him to a big stone at the end of the garden so he could sit on it and watch while we finished covering the seeds.

When I went to help him up I saw he was clutching something in his hand. I asked him what, and he showed me—five pumpkin seeds. With tears in my eyes, I grabbed the hoe and told him we would plant his seeds. He got so excited trying to put each seed in the right spot and covering them with loving pats.

Whenever they came, the first thing he asked about was his garden. The summer proved to be a dry, hot one and found Dan and I carrying water to the garden and an extra pail for the pumpkin.

The vine grew real well, and when they came in September he had two nice pumpkins on it. It was the first place he wanted to go. When he came in the house he said, "I'm going to call that big one Mr. Big."

The next day I decided to chop some weeds out of the vine and accidentally chopped the roots and Mr. Big died.

I felt so bad, and so did Dan. I knew I should tell Doug, but I kept putting it off, starting letters and tearing them up.

A week before Halloween, Doug called and said they were coming that weekend for his Mr. Big. He was so excited I couldn't tell him. I could still see him clutching those seeds, and the effort it took to plant them. As I turned from the phone with tears in my eyes I said to Dan, "We've got to go buy two pumpkins, and it will be our secret."

He said, "Wait for me!" When he came back he was carrying an armful of bittersweet vine. He said, "Mr. Big has to have some vines."

We went to a farmer that grew cow pumpkins and got the biggest one he had and one small one. Then with the aid of Scotch tape and glue, we were ready for Doug.

He didn't look at the vine, only the huge pumpkin. He wrapped his arms around it and said, "He's super."

With tears in our eyes we picked it for him and sat it on his dresser for the night.

Doug is gone now, but this is one of our happy memories. My husband asks me if I'm not sorry and ashamed to have fooled him and never told him the truth.

I say, "No. My lie never hurt him. It made him very, very happy."

As I said, I loved the story. How could I help it? And what a salable subject! Every magazine looks for seasonal material. Yet how many religious magazines are able to find appropriate stories with a Halloween theme?

Eva is a natural storyteller. The story flows. It is simple, clear, and moving. She starts at exactly the right place and carries through, using sharp images and alternating narration with dialogue. But the most impressive thing she has done is not apparent to the reader—she has *left out* material that does not further the story line. I happen to know that Doug was the youngest of three brothers, all with muscular dystrophy. This incurable and progressive disease first begins to affect a child at about the time he starts school, and from then on the muscles grow weaker and weaker until death eventually occurs. At the time of this story, Doug had one brother on crutches and one in a wheelchair. Each younger brother could see his own future mirrored in his next oldest sibling.

It must have been an almost irresistible temptation to Eva to bring these other beloved grandsons into the story, but she didn't do it. Instinctively she knew that they didn't belong there. This was the story of Doug and Mr. Big.

The changes I suggested that Eva make were small ones, and there were not many, but they were enough to make the difference between a rejection and a sale. This is what they were:

1. The addition of more live dialogue. For instance:

> Doug was curious about a plain envelope at the bottom of the pile.
> "What's this?" he asked.
> "Oh, those aren't anything," Dan told him. "Just some seeds I saved from last year's Halloween pumpkin."
> "Can we plant them?" Doug asked, his eyes brightening. "We could make them into jack-o-lanterns."
> "We don't have enough room, honey," I told him gently. "Things with vines need lots of growing space . . ."

2. Elimination of the fact that "Dan grabbed a package of watermelon seeds." After all, watermelons grow on vines too. It does seem a bit unfair to let Dan plant his watermelons while telling poor Doug that he can't plant his pumpkins.

3. Reducing to one occasion the times on which people had "tears in their eyes." In the original manuscript, this occurred four times. It's three times too many, especially in such a very short story. I'm sure that in reality there were tears in Eva's eyes a lot of the time when she observed Doug, but to mention this over and over again reduces the effectiveness of the image. Used in the final scene only—"With tears in our eyes we carried it in and set it on his dresser for the night"—it's very touching.

4. The smoothing out of a few awkward sentences. For example: "The summer proved to be a dry, hot one and found Dan and I carrying water to the garden and an extra pail for the pumpkin" was reworded to read, "The summer proved to be a dry, hot one, and Dan and I had to carry water to the garden constantly. Each time we took one extra pail, just for the pumpkins."

5. The story's ending. This is what bothered me most, especially for a religious publication. In the last paragraph it sounded as though Eva was applauding her own shrewdness. Here was an adult who put one over on a child. Even with love as the reason, it goes down wrong.

The altered ending, on the final draft of the manuscript, read as follows:

A week before Halloween, Doug phoned and told me his mother was driving him out that weekend for his Mr. Big. His voice sang at the prospect.

I still could not force myself to give him the news.

"I can't bear it," I said to Dan. "It's going to break his heart."

"We could buy a pumpkin," Dan suggested.

"It wouldn't be the same. It's Mr. Big that Doug wants."

"Well, let's give him Mr. Big then," Dan said determinedly. "One pumpkin looks like another."

"But he'll want to pick it himself! You know he will!" I said.

"Okay," Dan said. "Okay. You go buy the pumpkins and leave the rest to me."

There was something in his voice that kept me from asking questions. I went to a neighbor farmer who grew cow pumpkins and got the biggest one he had and one small one. When I got home I found Dan dragging a large bunch of bittersweet vine across the yard.

"Mr. Big has to have vines," he told me. He arranged them in the spot where the pumpkin vine had been, and with Scotch tape and glue he attached the two pumpkins. "Now," he said, "we're ready for Dougie."

Doug didn't look at the vine when he arrived the next morning, only at the pumpkin. His illness had progressed to the point where he was unable even to attempt to lift it, so Dan had to do it for him. Carefully, Dan placed the pumpkin in the little boy's lap, and Doug's arms went around it.

"He's super!" he exclaimed. "Mr. Big's just super!"

With tears in our eyes we carried it in and set it on his dresser for the night.

Doug is gone now, unable to make it through his teenage years. But that Halloween is a happy memory we cherish. I relive it each October when Dan, now grown, brings his own small children to look over the current pumpkin crop.

"Let's find us a Mr. Big," he says, and I remember Doug's proud face and joyful smile. And I remember, too, that moment when I looked at my 10-year-old son and realized, for the first time, the kind of man he was going to be.

The basic facts of the story remain unchanged, but this new ending does two things. First it switches the emphasis from Eva's cleverness to Dan's. This way when she describes the kindly deception she doesn't sound self-congratulating. Second, it gives us an upbeat conclusion. The original story left us sunk in sorrow, with Doug's death a heartbreaking finality. With this second version, we are left with an image of the live Dan, celebrating with his own young children, with love and family solidarity surviving.

What sort of questions should you ask yourself before starting your rewrite? Here are a few:

Is this story shaped right? Does it build to make its point? Is the hook interesting enough to intrigue the reader? Is there a smooth transition between the hook and the body of the article? Am I making all the points I want to make in the right order? Have I put in excess material that does not contribute? Does my story flow smoothly and easily and naturally from one scene to another? Does the climax come too abruptly so that I need more buildup? Or do I wait too long so that the reader is worn out before he reaches it? Do I hit the climax hard enough to make it worth the reader's effort to get there? Do I wind things up neatly so that the reader is left with a feeling of satisfaction?

You may have noticed that I have been using the words "story" and "article" interchangeably. This is because these same questions apply to both fiction and articles. The basics of construction in writing are as constant as the basics in any other kind of creative building. Whether you're making a boat or a coffee table, you have to get it in balance or it's going to fall over.

In my own case, I usually put a story through two stages of revision. The second is when I try to make it beautiful. Now the questions I ask myself concern smoothness and polish:

Are the anecdotes appropriate and well handled? Is the dialogue natural? Does my story read easily with neither choppy paragraphs nor long unbroken ones? Have I used the best words possible to express my meanings? Have I used a favorite word too often? Am I overworking my adjectives and adverbs? Are there spots where I have been too wordy? Are my sentences grammatically correct and in a style in keeping with the sort of piece I am writing? How is my spelling?

All in all, is this the best, most polished job I am capable of doing? Am I proud of the result? Is there any way that I can improve upon it?

It is far easier to pinpoint the flaws in somebody else's work than in your own. Sometimes even long-time professionals get so close to stories they are working on that they are unable to assess them objectively. All the while I was critiquing my students' work and demanding rewrites, editors of national magazines were critiquing *my* articles and on many occasions demanding rewrites of *me*.

When Tony Hillerman introduced me to university teaching, he opened more doors for me than either of us realized. Back in my early years I had been so excited about getting out of high school so I could start "really living" that I had shrugged off any suggestion that further education might be good for me. If I was going to be a writer, I ought to be *writing*, not studying; if I was going to be an adult, I ought to be *married!*

That represented rebellion in my generation. Today's youth may not be leaping into marriage, but the revolution against regimented learning is very much alive. Our music major, Robin, dropped out of college to sing in nightclubs, and Kerry, our actress, dropped out to seek her fortune in Hollywood.

"Twelve years of school is enough! It's time to get moving!" they informed us. I remember the feeling—yes, I remember it well.

But two more decades of living can make a difference. As I watched and listened to my students, I began to realize that a lot of interesting activity was going on behind the adobe walls of our university. Philosophy, history, psychology, and literature started to sound pretty exciting, and I decided to take a course or two just for fun. It proved to be more than simply that. A study of literature has exposed me to the works of writers whose abilities so surpass mine that I now have new goals of excellence to strive for. Classes in philosophy have deepened my thinking and helped me to enrich my characterization. Courses in history have given me background for novels still to be written, which I would otherwise never have considered attempting. Most valuable of all have been the psychology classes, for by understanding better why people become what they are and what influences them to act in certain ways, I find it far easier to create on paper people who ring true.

Practical knowledge came in the form of a photography class which paid for itself almost immediately by enabling me to take pictures to accompany my articles and to illustrate a book of poems for small children, *From Spring to Spring*.

The surprising part is that it has cost me nothing to go to college. I've been more than able to pay for tuition and books by writing about the things I've learned. Psychology classes were particularly fruitful. There are a million how-to articles waiting to be written on such subjects as how to make marriage work, be a good friend, raise children, handle aging parents, deal with emotional crises, and break bad habits. I made my first major sale in Psychology 101, where we were training rats to run through mazes. The rats did what we wanted much more willingly and were happier, better-adjusted animals when rewarded for a good performance than when punished for a poor one. During the course we were taught to transfer this principle to dealing with humans, and I wrote an article about this for a major women's magazine.

With this success behind me, I eagerly signed up for a class on the Psychology of Education, which provided material for "Those IQ Scores—What Do They Really Mean?" for *The Woman*. Other classes produced material for more articles, and eventually I even managed to sell my Milton term paper to *Writer's Digest*, where it appeared in April, 1975, in condensed form as their "Rejection Slip of the Month."

As a grand climax to my college money-making career, I wrote up the account of my graduation at middle age for the "It Happened to Me" feature in *Good Housekeeping*. It was published along with a photo of me, cheering with joy, in my cap and gown, and another of the entire family enjoying my triumph. I feel good about that story. I like to think that it may have inspired other housewives to return to school and experience the same satisfactions I did.

I also feel good about the fact that Robin and Kerry eventually decided to follow in their mother's footsteps. Both have now graduated from the University of New Mexico with degrees in television journalism.

> **. . . .All the while I was critiquing my students' work and demanding rewrites, editors of national magazines were critiquing *my* articles and on many occasions demanding rewrites of *me* . . .**

Dear Lois:

Please forgive the delay in getting back to you on your piece on "Ten Sticky Money Problems and How to Solve Them," but I've been up to my ears in deadline projects.

I've discussed the manuscript with my colleagues here at *Woman's Day*, and though we find it well-written, it is not quite as helpful as we'd hoped. I'm sure you can fix it, but I'm afraid I must ask for more work.

Your "board of experts" is interesting, but not what I had in mind. As described, it sounds a little too limited and casual. It's fine to say you got your solutions from an informal poll of friends, but let your readers know also that you discussed the situations with psychologists.

The situations themselves are generally very good, but the stickiness is not always clear. It would help to introduce each section with a typical situation that makes women feel resentful or uncomfortable.

I'm not enthusiastic about all your suggestions for handling these situations. We don't need opposing points of view in each case, nor should you include suggestions that seem impractical. The fact that one of your board of experts suggested a solution is not sufficient; it must be workable for most readers. For example, it's not helpful to mention that one of the women questioned says nothing when a friend borrows money and forgets to return it.

Under transportation expenses, you've considered two extremes—the cross country trip and the short hop across town—but ignored the situation that causes the most trouble, the person who regularly chauffeurs a friend on jaunts of 25 to 100 miles. Maybe they drive to vacation houses in the same area or go antiquing together on weekends, but only one friend has a car. None of us minds paying the bills for a single trip, but when you drive every weekend and your friend never offers to help with expenses it gets annoying.

I'd rather substitute another "sticky situation" for #10, the one about being overwhelmed by Christmas expenses. This seems too seasonal. (We also covered the same problem in a previous Christmas issue.)

I've made additional comments and suggestions on the manuscript itself. Despite the length of all this, I think the piece should be easy to fix; if I didn't, I wouldn't be spending this much effort critiquing it. As usual, I'm playing devil's advocate in an effort to make the article as strong and helpful as possible. If you have any questions—or disagree with any of my suggestions—don't hesitate to call me collect.

I look forward to seeing the revisions.

Best regards,
Rebecca Greer, Articles Editor

Using your life experiences to inspire others

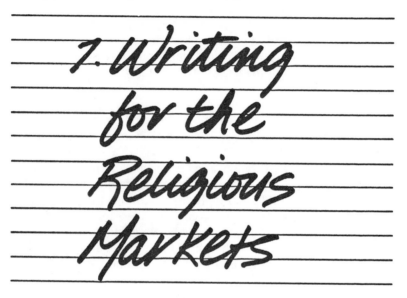

7. Writing for the Religious Markets

I am going to tell you a horror story.

The year after Don and I were married, I decided to tackle a new project and write first-person feature stories for some of the high-pay consumer magazines. These features followed a regular pattern—the protagonist, usually a housewife, faced a problem, the more devastating the better, and after reaching a crisis point managed to solve it, thereby helping and inspiring the reader to face and solve problems of her own. The stories were published anonymously.

The problem I wrote about first was one with which I was familiar, that of a divorced woman trying to support and raise three children alone. The basic situation was the one I myself had lived through, but, knowing the story would not have a by-line, I felt free to embellish it as much as I wanted. I made the divorcee an only child who had had polio as a baby and had been spoiled and coddled by her parents until she was all but helpless. When her husband left her, she could hardly manage to lock up the house at night, much less manage a one-parent household.

I mailed the story off to a popular women's magazine.

The features editor liked it but was not enthusiastic about having a viewpoint character who was divorced.

"Our readers are conservative," she wrote me. "They would relate better if the woman were a widow."

Well, that was fine with me. For the amount this magazine paid, I was more than willing to make the poor thing a widow or anything else for that matter. So I rewrote the article and submitted it again.

It was rejected.

So, there I was with a story I had invested a good deal of time and effort in with no reimbursement.

I got out *Writer's Market* and leafed through it in search of a second market. Finally, I found a listing for a publication that wanted "first person, inspirational stories about people who face and overcome problems."

Perfect! I mailed off my article, and back came a check for $100. This was much less than I would have received if I had sold to the first market, but it was far better than nothing. I cashed the check and bought new curtains for the kitchen.

Several months later, I received a letter from the publication that had bought my story, asking if I would send them a snapshot to go with the article. This set me back. Still, I decided, why not? I had never heard of the magazine and it wasn't to be seen on any of our local newsstands. I decided it was probably some little regional story paper that never got any further than the town in which it was published. Digging a snapshot out of the family album, I mailed it to them and tossed the whole thing out of my mind.

Until the article was published.

The magazine was *Guideposts*. There was no reason for the publication to be on newsstands, for everybody in the United States except Don and me apparently had a subscription. The story was not published anonymously. There was my name in big black letters with "Albuquerque, New Mexico" printed beneath it, and there, enlarged and totally recognizable, was my face, smiling pluckily out at a couple of million readers.

It was instant notoriety. No story I wrote before or after had received so much attention. Somebody called the *Albuquerque Journal* and an announcement of the story's publication appeared on the women's page. People would stop me as I walked down the street and ask, "Aren't you the little widow lady in this month's issue of *Guideposts*?"

I would cringe and nod and watch their eyes fill with horrified disbelief. I was eight and a half months pregnant at the time.

Letters poured in to *Guideposts* from shocked readers who were canceling their subscriptions. Equally shocked letters from *Guideposts* came airmail to me. How could I have done this to them? I had ruined their reputation! Readers who had formerly trusted the magazine had now lost their faith! How could I have instigated such a deplorable fraud!

I, who had never really thought of it as fraud—who actually had never thought much about it at all—shuddered each time another envelope bearing the *Guideposts* letterhead dropped through the mail slot in the door. Not only did I feel terribly guilty for having created such a situation, I was sure I was going to be sued. Imagine winning a law suit initiated by Norman Vincent Peale!

This story could have had a sadder ending, for the worst did not occur. The editors of *Guideposts*, while they never totally forgave me, decided to chalk the whole thing up as "a learning experience for us all." I knew what *I* had learned, but I was never certain what it was that *they* had gotten out of it until a student of mine sold her own story to *Guideposts*.

Along with her acceptance letter there was a request for her written assurance that the story was absolutely factual, as there had been an embarrassing incident once when an unscrupulous contributor had sold them a fictionalized story disguised as fact.

"Can you imagine anyone doing such a thing!" my student exclaimed.

I was grateful that she did not expect an answer.

The *Guideposts* incident was my initiation into the world of religious publications. Until then I had never considered them a market. The fact that they are not sold on the stands, but are distributed by subscription and through the churches, makes them a kind of publication that you can easily overlook. Still, when you stop to consider that each denomination publishes its own church-related material that ranges from adult magazines to carry-home Sunday school papers for toddlers, you begin to realize that this represents a large market indeed.

The religious publications are a mecca for the personal experience writer. Have you ever had a problem and found strength to solve it through your faith in God? Have you faced a temptation and managed to reject it? Has there been a turning point in your life when you realized you were on the wrong track, did an about-face, and started over in a new and better direction? Have you ever been through a rough time and come out on the other side of it, stronger and more self-reliant than you were before?

If so, you have a story for one of the inspirational publications. What are the requirements for writing for religious magazines?

First, as I learned the hard way, you need to be honest. If you submit fiction, it must be so labeled. If you submit articles, they must be factually correct. This does not mean that you cannot arrange the elements of your story in such a way that they build to a strong conclusion. It does not mean that you cannot emphasize the things you want emphasized and omit the extraneous material which doesn't further the movement of the story. It does not mean that you can't insert dialogue into areas where it would be natural, even though you may not remember actual conversations word for word.

What it does mean is that if you are divorced you don't represent yourself as a widow, and if you are married and pregnant, you had better not write your article as though you are single.

Second, you should know enough about the beliefs of various religious denominations so that you do not violate their principles with your submissions. My first submission to *Home Life* was returned for revision when I thoughtlessly mentioned a family dinner at which wine was served.

The editor's letter was gentle but firm:

"We admire your honesty in admitting that you drank a glass of wine on this occasion, but we would prefer to have you delete this sentence from your otherwise fine and inspirational story."

Home Life is a Southern Baptist publication. Such a reference would not have bothered the editors of a Catholic magazine.

The people in *Home Life* articles drink coffee by the gallon. Husbands and wives are always sitting together at the breakfast table to iron out family problems "over a second cup of coffee." Not so the people in the articles in *The New Era*, a Mormon publication. Nor do these people imbibe tea or cocoa.

I have had articles returned from Christian fundamentalist publications because they were accompanied by photographs in which little girls were wearing overalls ("We do not condone the wearing of slacks or shorts by women") or because teenage boys had hair that hung "lower than the ear lobe." Some of my pictures were rejected by a Mennonite magazine because women in them were wearing jewelry. A Seventh-day Adventist magazine rejected a set of Christmas pictures because "although we find the photos quite intriguing, we don't use Christmas scenes with gaudy tinsel and elaborately decorated trees."

How do you learn the requirements and taboos for such an assortment of magazines?

The only way is to read them. Names and addresses of most of the religious publications that accept freelance material can be found in *Writer's Market*, and they will almost all send you sample copies and "guide sheets for writers" on request. One thing you need to be aware of is the fact that these magazines tend to purchase seasonal material as much as a year ahead, so the Christmas story you submit in November, if it is accepted, won't appear in print for thirteen months. In this way they differ from the consumer publications which buy six to eight months ahead.

In writing for the religious publications, you can shape your personal experiences to fit all the same forms that are appropriate for the general consumer magazines:

The Personality Piece. This will be a profile of an inspiring person you know who is involved in helping others or who has beaten great odds in order to make of himself the sort of person he feels God wants him to be.

An example: "Brother Mathias: Forever Flexible," by my student Pat Archibeck. Pat's story about seventy-eight-year-old Brother Mathias and his home for retarded men was published in *Columbia*.

Drama in Real Life. This will be a true, dramatic, human-interest story about someone who has survived an ordeal with God's help. One magazine suggests, "Find someone with a problem. Then tell us how he solves it."

An example: The article one of my students wrote for *Living With Teenagers* about her experience with a daughter who was a drug addict.

The Opinion Piece. This can be about a social issue or moral problem. You must be careful here to make certain that your "opinion" conforms with the doctrine of the faith.

An example: "God Belongs in the Public Schools," by a student who is battling for morning prayers in the school her children attend.

The How-To. This will be about such things as "how to inspire and excite the children in your Sunday school class" or "how I stopped smoking" or "how I keep my teenagers from leaving the faith."

The Direct Personal Experience Piece. For the straw-into-gold-writer, this is the easiest way to break into the inspirational publications. All you have to do is to tell simply and sincerely about an event in your life that was meaningful to your development as a person.

An example of a personal experience article is "The Day That Changed My Life," by Mary Johnson, a housewife-writer who took my class several years ago and has since sold a number of articles and stories to religious publications. This was Mary's first article, and she sold it to *Home Life*. With her permission, I am going to use it to demonstrate how such an article can be put together.

Here is Mary's hook:

My arms were being punched with needles. Bottles hung above me. White-coated people scurried about. The noise of voices, clicking of equipment and moans of other patients hurt my ears.

The lights were bright, and my eyes burned. A doctor hovered just above my head, looking peculiar upside down.

I formed my words carefully and asked with simple curiosity, not fear, "Am I going to die?"

Directive statement:

I had never really thought of death in relation to myself. I had never really thought of much in relation to myself, for that matter. The routine of caring for a husband, three children, and a house consumed all my time and energy. Gradually boredom had crept upon me, and lately each day seemed a gray span of time to be endured. I would wash a pail of diapers, only to face another pailful the next morning. Cleaning house seemed futile with two toddlers trailing along behind me, messing up as fast as I cleaned. Washing dishes was a chore I detested.

My whole life had become an endless drudgery. I felt robotlike, mechanical. "I want a drink"—get child a drink. "Read to me"—read child a book. "My knee hurts"—get child a bandage. Demand, response; demand, response.

Let's look at what Mary has done here, because it's a technique that is often used in magazine writing, in fiction as well as in personal experience articles, and I'm going to be referring to it in later chapters.

For her hook, Mary has selected a scene that takes place at a suspenseful spot *right before the story's climax*. She has left us with a cliff-hanger. A woman, our heroine, is in the operating room, asking. "Am I going to die?" Well, is she? We assume not, since the story is written in the first person and it's difficult for a corpse to get much done at the typewriter; but we do want to know what is going to happen next, how badly our narrator is hurt, and whether she will ever be able to live a normal life. Knowing she has us well hooked, Mary very deliberately leaves us hanging there and makes her directive statement. She does this in a couple of paragraphs during which she lets us know what the story is going to be about—the narrator's boredom and dissatisfaction with her life routine. How will this be overcome? We don't know. We are going to read on in order to find out.

Now, with the reader hooked and the situation established, Mary goes into a *flashback*. She flashes back in time to a point well before her hook and gives us a chronological account of how she came to be in the situation in which we find her at the story's opening:

> I had considered going to work to relieve the terrible boredom. The morning of the wreck I had scanned the want ads, toying with the idea of actually applying.
>
> I was interrupted by, "Mommy, see what I made?" It was Andy, three, proudly displaying a tiny bouquet picked from a large, expensive centerpiece of dried flowers. I shrieked when I realized what he had done. His proud look turned to terror and tears as I turned my wrath on him.
>
> "Andy, you have ruined Mommy's beautiful centerpiece. How could you!" I lashed out at him....Nancy, with a gentleness learned from twelve years of avoiding my outbursts, came in and said, "Mama, what time is the party?" I suddenly remembered we had been invited to a birthday party that afternoon.

From here Mary moves us along step by step as the mother gets her children ready for the party, resenting each bit of work involved.

"Mama, what should I wear?" Nancy asks.

"Wear whatever you want," snaps her mother. "Don't expect me to always tell you what to wear. You ought to be able to do that by yourself."

Eventually we reach the point where they are driving down the expressway en route to the party at last, and:

> . . . a light-colored station wagon driven by a 16-year-old boy careened across the median and crashed head-on into our car.
>
> Waking in my hospital bed the next morning . . .

And she has brought us back to the scene where we came in. From here on, Mary tells the remainder of the story chronologically. The children have survived the crash with only minor injuries, but Mary herself is badly hurt and has come close to death:

> But here I was, alive and wondering why! From that moment I knew God had spared my life for a reason. I knew that going to work was not the answer to my boredom but that a whole new outlook on life would be needed.

This, then, is the turning point of the story. After her release from the hospital, Mary is confined for two months to her bed, and a kind and capable cleaning woman named Inez does all the things that Mary has formerly had to do and has so much resented.

Lying in bed, listening to the normal household sounds, Mary wonders whether she will ever again have the strength to take over her old chores and realizes how important her role in filling the everyday needs of her family actually was to her.

When her youngest child comes to her bedside and asks her to read to him, Mary finds that her eyes will not focus well enough to make out the words, and Inez picks up the child and takes him off to a rocking chair for a reading time. (Mary has paved the way for this scene by inserting the plea, "Read to me," earlier in the story as an example of "demand, response; demand, response.")

When Nancy has her thirteenth birthday party, it is Inez who helps her select which dress she will wear (a situation Mary has also prepared us for by having an earlier scene in which she tells her daughter, "Don't expect me to always tell you what to wear").

These foreshadowings of things to come are called "plants." Mary has "planted" items that will be echoed in the story, and because of the plants, the later events have meaning. Without the mother's previous reaction to the requests of her children established in our minds, we would not react so strongly to the fact that she now wants to do things for them and is unable to.

For her conclusion, Mary solves her problem:

> I wept as I came to realize how fully blessed I was with a husband and children and a home to care for. A certain joy now fills my heart as I perform even the most routine tasks around our home.

She winds up her story with a short scene in the backyard in which she is digging and planting flowers with her six-year-old who looks up and says, "I'm glad you're my mommy," and Mary answers, "I am too, honey," and breathes a soft, "Thank you, God."

The subtle use of the planting of live flowers in this final scene contrasts effectively with the early scene in which the dried flowers had so much meaning.

The story is an account of a true event in Mary's life. She actually was in an accident such as the one she described; and she really was confined in bed for a length of time and gained new insight into the validity of her value system. However, in telling the story she followed a road map that led to the conclusion she wanted to make and utilized only those scenes that would build to the climax.

Let's pretend Mary was going in another direction with her article and had no intention of submitting it to a religious publication. Let's say that the conclusion she wanted to reach was that the proper use of safety belts in cars can save lives. Would she use the same scenes?

No, out would go Andy and the flowers and Nancy and the dress. There would be no reason to include them. Nor would there be any sense in describing Mary's dislike of her house-wife existence. Although she could still use the dramatic account of the automobile accident, the stress would be on safety problems. She would build toward the climax using scenes involving the safety belts, the kids fussing over being forced to wear them, Mary's insistence, and perhaps the fact that she never bothered buckling on her own. The come-to-realize conclusion would be that the extra time and bother of snapping on the awkward things were more than worth it when she considered the fact that they saved her children's lives.

The facts would be the same. The emphasis would shift. And the resulting article would go to an entirely different sort of publication.

"The Day That Changed My Life" is based on an incident of drama. Not all of us have been through the sort of dreadful experience Mary has, but we have all had turning points in our lives, times when we reexamined our value systems and matured in the process. These low-key stories can be moving and inspiring in themselves.

. . . low-key stories can be moving and inspiring in themselves . . .

My parents did not give us a present on the occasion of our wedding.

"We want to wait," they said, "until we find exactly the right thing."

I was their only daughter and the oldest of their children. It took them three years to select the gift.

It was a silver tea service. Heavy. Ornate. As far as I was concerned, utterly useless. We were the wine and spaghetti generation. Nobody we knew gave tea parties. I stood there gazing at that mass of metal, and I thought I was going to cry.

"It's—lovely," I managed to say. "But, you shouldn't—"

"My grandmother had one just like it," Mother told me. "She left it to my mother who left it to me. I don't want you to have to wait until I am gone to have one of your own."

We were very young and very broke, and there were dozens of things we needed desperately.

"Think what they must have spent!" my husband groaned. "For what that cost, we could have gotten a washer or a used car or paid off the hospital bill for the baby!"

We could not return it, for it had been purchased at an auction. Like it or not, we were the owners of a seven-piece tea service.

Ours was a too young marriage that did not last. There came a day when I found myself facing the loneliness and problems of a divorcee. With no training, I struggled at one low-pay job after another in frustration and near despair. The baby spent his days in a nursery and the little girls wore secondhand dresses. Dinner was often peanut butter sandwiches.

But on a card table in our tiny apartment there sat a silver tea service that would have graced a queen's palace. I looked at it often during those years in a way I had not looked before. I saw in my mind the long, slim hands of the Duncan women pouring tea—my great-grandmother in a mansion on a southern plantation, my grandmother who gave up a career as a concert pianist to follow her love to a little town in the Ozarks, my own mother during the Depression, hocking the furniture to put food on the table.

She did not sell her silver.

Neither did I.

There is something about having a thing of loveliness in your home that forces you to try to live up to it. Even worn out from a deadly day of writing advertising copy, you take the time to make that extra effort. To comb the children's hair. To put flowers on the table. To serve those sandwiches by candlelight. To play music. To ask friends over.

To pour tea.

Those days are over now. I am happily remarried, and those first three children have a younger brother and sister. I have never given a tea party, and I don't suppose I ever will.

But the service sits on a buffet in our dining room. It will go, one day, to my oldest daughter. She will undoubtedly be even less enthusiastic about receiving it than I was. It will look a bit out of place in a commune or a Peace Corps hut in Africa or wherever she sets up housekeeping with the lover of her choice.

But you cannot look ahead. There may come a time for her, as there did for me, when she feels a need for something that her own generation cannot provide for her.

The strength of family. A sense of dignity.

A touch of grace.

("A Touch of Grace," *Scope*)

8. Writing for the Confessions

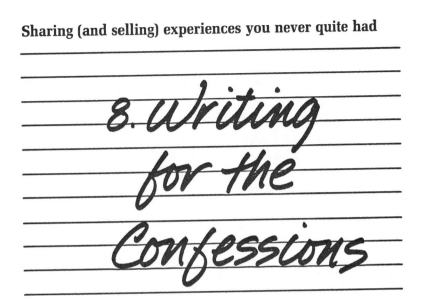

When my first marriage ended, I went out at age twenty-seven to find my first job. This was not easy, as I had nothing to recommend me—no college degree, no business training, no work experience. I was hired at last by a small advertising agency to answer the telephone, run errands and write occasional copy. My monthly salary was $275, which I hoped to supplement by writing articles and stories in the evenings.

That was wishful thinking. By the time I left work and picked up Brett at his nursery, collected the girls at their after-school sitter's, came home and cooked dinner and spent some time with the children, got them bathed and bedded down, cleaned up the apartment, did the laundry and got things in order for the next day, I was too exhausted to write a letter to my parents, much less something suitable for publication. I sat like a zombie in front of the typewriter and often ended up asleep with my head on the keyboard.

Because of this I was constantly looking for extra ways to earn money. On my lunch hour I entered contests. One was sponsored by the Florida Development Commission and was for "happy snapshots taken while on vacation in Florida." I had visited my parents in Florida the summer before and entered a "happy snapshot" of Brett, age three, jumping into the water. Another was for "the most frightening experience of your life in one hundred words or less." I entered that one several times.

One day I came home from work after an especially tiring day, gave the mail a quick once-over and, finding nothing there but bills and ads, tossed it into a heap on the coffee table. The following evening I picked it up again to give it a second look before throwing it away. There was a letter I had thought was an ad because it started "Dear Reader." Now I saw that it was not an ad at all.

"Dear Reader," it said. "It is my pleasant duty to inform you that your 'frightening experience' has won first prize in *True Story's* contest. Your check is enclosed."

Enclosed in what? I regarded the pile on the coffee table with horror. Robin, whose job it was to take out the trash each day, had been conscientious. She had thrown away the envelope.

Our apartment was part of a huge, low-cost complex. There must have been fifty garbage cans lined up out back. The children and I got a flashlight and, starting at one end of the row, went rooting through all of them. Finally, halfway down about the fifteenth can, buried under somebody's leftover spaghetti, we found the envelope. Inside, there was a check for $500.

Five hundred dollars was almost twice what I was earning each month at the agency, and by working away from home I had the expenses of a nursery for Brett, an after-school sitter for the girls, commuting and panty hose for myself. I made my decision quickly. If there was this kind of money to be made by writing for the confessions, there was no sense spending my days writing advertising copy. One thing that made this decision easier was a phone call from the Florida Development Commission informing me that my "happy snapshot" had won first prize: a live, trained porpoise from Marineland, Florida. At my strangled gasp of horror (I had a vision of the thing arriving in a crate of salt water and having to be kept in the bathtub). I was offered a chance to sell the porpoise back to Marineland for $1,000. So we did have this nest egg to draw upon while I taught myself the craft of confession writing.

I quit my job, went to the newsstand and bought every confession magazine on the rack (there were twenty-four of them, if I remember correctly), and read each one from cover to cover. By the time I had finished this cram course, I had a pretty good idea of how a confession story was put together.

From then on, every Monday morning, I got up, brushed my teeth, and sat down at the typewriter to confess. My first sale was to *True Story* and was about my kleptomania. I described how I would walk through the supermarket, dropping cans of sardines and mushrooms and other overpriced goodies into my purse until finally I was apprehended by the store detective and forced to see the error of my ways.

I had never actually done this, of course. Yet—you can experience things vicariously. I did know what it was like to lust after mushrooms. And smoked oysters. And rib lamb chops. And artichoke hearts. And to stand in a deserted aisle with your mouth watering for such luxuries with just enough cash in your purse to cover the cost of a package of macaroni. It is not too great a mental step to move from temptation-resisted to temptation-given-in-to.

I called that story "I Took What I Wanted." It was rejected several times before it sold. Each time I read it over, tried to analyze what the problem was, and rewrote it. The resulting sale brought me $300 and a letter asking me to contribute more stories.

From then on, I wrote a story a week. Not every one sold, but most did. Soon we were living better than we ever had before. We gave up our awful apartment and bought a house. The little girls took dancing lessons and piano lessons and ice skating lessons, while Brett went to a private kindergarten. We ate steak at least once a week and sometimes oftener. And I served mushrooms on it!

Some sample stories from those productive years:

"We Killed Our Baby"—Our colicky baby was wrecking

our marriage by crying every night when my husband and I were trying to make love, so I began putting paregoric in her evening bottle. Not knowing about this, my husband got the same idea; we double-dosed her, and that was it for little Doreen.

"Twenty-Nine and the Mother of Two, I Wanted an Affair with a Teenage Boy"—This one made all my friends who had teenage boys very nervous.

"Your Husband Has Another Woman"—Unhappy in my own marriage, I set out to wreck the marriages of everyone else in the neighborhood by writing poison pen letters to smug, self-confident wives.

"Afraid to Tell Him I Was Half a Woman"—About my breast surgery.

"I Made My Son a Daughter"—I won't go into what this was about.

"Two Men Claim Me As Their Wife"—About my bigamy.

Once I got the formula under my belt, I got very good and very fast at writing confessions. I could start one Monday morning and have the final draft completed and in the mail by Wednesday evening. This left me the remainder of the week to work on my major, long-term project, which was the writing of teenage novels. I counted on the confession stories to cover our living expenses while the books, with their low but continual royalties, would be my insurance against the years ahead.

After two years on this schedule, I began to run out of sins to write about. Glued to my typewriter, I had had no time for doing research. One day my brother, who worked for the government, took pity on my situation.

"Get a babysitter," he told me, "and I'll take you out to the base for Happy Hour tonight and introduce you to some of the bachelor types who work in missile design. They'll tell you about sins you never dreamed of!"

That evening I met Don Arquette.

Don and I knew each other two years before we were married. He won't admit it, but I think the reason for this is that every time he began to think about proposing, another confession story would come out and I would wave it proudly in his face. The week he did propose, *Personal Romances* published "I Carry That Dreadful Disease," and he almost reneged. On our wedding day, out came "Can He Bear to Touch Me on Our Wedding Night?" confessing that I was nothing but scar tissue from my neck to my knees. But he did go through with the ceremony and adopted the children, and another set of personal experiences began for us all.

There are rules and boundaries in writing confessions, just as there are in any other kind of writing. Confessions are read primarily by an audience of women. The majority of these women have at the most a high-school education, marry early, have "jobs" rather than "careers," and pour their whole beings into their role as wives and mothers.

These are women who feel deeply, and their approach to life is emotional rather than intellectual. When they love, they love hard, and they expect to be loved hard in return. When they are sad, they weep openly and unashamedly. When they are mad, they yell and throw things. The problems they face in their daily lives are centered around their homes and families. They are religious, hardworking, concerned about the well-being of their children and the stability of their home life. They have strict ideas of right and wrong, and though they can sympathize with a heroine who makes a mistake or is forced into wrongdoing, they cannot condone malice and they want to see right prevail. They do not live easy lives, these readers, and when they read they want to see women like themselves, facing and conquering problems even greater than their own. When you think of it this way, there is a surprisingly thin line between the confession story and the personal experience piece written for a religious publication. The main difference is that the religious article is based on fact and the confession, though many readers think that the stories in these magazines are true, is fiction.

I learned by experience how to write confession stories, and because I was self-taught I made many mistakes at first. Let me describe some of the stories that were rejected:

"I Took What I Wanted." This was my first story, about the housewife who becomes a shoplifter in order to provide her family with things her lazy husband does not earn enough to buy.

This came back several times before it finally sold, because the wife's motive for stealing was not strong enough to be acceptable. Confession readers live without luxuries and do not turn to lives of crime—why can't our heroine? The story sold at last when I revised it so that the wife was stealing in order to get food and medication for her deprived children.

"I Hid My Children." A young divorcee, unable to afford a babysitter, leaves her children alone while she dates a man who does not want a family.

Why didn't this sell? Because, to confession readers, their children are the most important thing in life. They cannot forgive any mother who neglects her youngsters. I was able to sell this only after I revised the story so that the mother thought a babysitter would be arriving momentarily and planned for the children to be alone for only a few minutes.

"I Can't Let Him See Me Now." A beautiful New York model survives an accident which badly scars her face and makes it impossible for her to continue her career.

What was wrong here? I skimped on my background material. The confession reader could not relate to the glamour of the setting. When I showed how our heroine worked her way up from high-school prom queen to become a model and—after the accident—had her return to her hometown and refall in love with her former boyfriend, this barrier was passed.

"I Can't Give Up My Job—Even for My Baby." A girl who has worked doing layouts for an advertising agency is miserable and bored when her husband insists that she stop working and stay at home with a new baby.

What was wrong? At the time I wrote this, it was inconceivable to most confession readers that a mother would choose to work if she didn't have to. An editor at Charlton Publications tells me that today, as a result of the women's liberation movement, this story would sell.

There are a few definite, never-to-be-broken rules in confession writing. Stories must always be written in the first person and in most cases the narrator should be a woman. The style should be natural and conversational, the pace fast, the emotion violent. The protagonist is a basically good person who makes a mistake, suffers, faces the dramatic end result of her mistake, and changes for the better. The "sin" must be committed for understandable reasons—love, pride, fear—not for greed, lust, or the conscious desire to hurt. The story must end with the narrator realizing her mistakes, sincerely regretting them, and either rectifying them or emerging determined to do better in the future.

There is a strong parallel between the confession story and the inspirational personal experience piece. The construction of the confession follows closely that of Mary Johnson's religious article, "The Day That Changed My Life." Let's look at the two of them and compare:

The confession usually opens with a dramatic hook scene immediately before the main action of the story. As with Mary's article, we see our heroine facing a terrible problem. Then, also as in Mary's story, we usually go into a flashback to show how the narrator got into this fix, work our way back to the opening scene, and go on chronologically from there.

The flashback is a necessary part of the confession story because it provides us with a look at the background of the narrator, so that the reader can understand what makes her the way she is. It is here that a writer must draw upon all that he has learned about human nature from his own past relationships in order to provide the sort of history that our heroine requires. When she makes her mistake, we want the reader to regard her with sympathy rather than scorn.

"What you're doing is wrong," we want her to think, "but, you poor girl, after all you've been through, I can see why it is that you're doing it. If I'd been influenced by all the things I learned about by reading the flashback, I might be out doing exactly what you're doing now."

This empathy makes it possible for the reader to care about the narrator, no matter what she does, and to care about what happens to her. The average reader is not going to be receptive to the protagonist who has an affair with somebody else's husband. "You little slut!" she will think. "You deserve whatever awful punishment you get!" But in our flashback we can go back to the time our heroine was a homely child, constantly rejected by her parents who loved a prettier sister better. We can show her to the reader as she reaches her teens and sits home in her bedroom night after night while luckier girls go to parties and dances: we can show her saving her hard-earned money to buy her father a birthday present only to have him tell her he doesn't like it: we can show the agonies she goes through hungering for affection and a feeling of self-worth and having it constantly denied her.

By the time we bring our reader back up to the point where we came in—the hook—in which our heroine is about to fall into her married lover's arms—we don't have a "slut" any longer, but a pathetic, gullible, emotionally starved young woman who has just heard the words "I love you" for the first time in her life from a man who swears that he and his wife haven't touched each other for years and stay together only for the sake of the children.

Our reader's heart melts. She may not condone, but she understands. Because of this, she will read the story all the way through to find out how it ends and whether or not our foolish-but-golden-hearted girl ever does find happiness.

What sorts of problems can we give our heroines? There are trends in those as well as in everything else. Some problems come into vogue and seem to hit all the confession magazines at one time. These magazines mirror whatever is currently in the news. At the time of the first heart-transplant operation, twenty stories must have come out with the theme, "I Sold My Baby's Heart." During a time of race riots, stories about mixed marriages became the "in" thing. More recently, sex-change operations became front-page news, and in the confessions we find "My Husband Is Our Son's Mother" and "Can I Tell My Wife I Am Really Her Sister?" "Dear Abby," "Ann Landers," and other advice columns provide endless situations the confession writer can utilize. Each letter they print has a story behind it, and if you can't figure it out, you can use the letter as a jump-off point and invent it.

One important thing in confession writing is to take each story seriously as you write it. This cannot be done tongue in cheek. Your readers aren't stupid. They recognize insincerity, and it infuriates them. They believe, or want to believe, that every story they read is a true account written by the story's heroine. To write that way, the author has to put herself fully into the story—in the heroine's skin—and stay there, experiencing her emotions and reacting to them.

This isn't difficult to do if the situations we write about are offshoots of our own experiences. The problems faced by confession-story heroines are no different from those of any other woman. Who among us has not made a mistake and suffered because of it? My own life has been pretty conventional, but my Lord, when I think back upon the mistakes I've managed to make, I either have to burst into tears or run to the typewriter. If you do happen to be one of those special people, blessed with a life of perfection (I did have one student who represented herself that way—a perfect woman with a perfect husband and two perfect daughters and a whole circle of perfect friends—the whole class hated her) what about your sister Martha? And cousin Jane? And your high school classmates? And the woman next door? You would never mention them by name, of course, and would change all details, but you can still ask yourself: "If they were to confess to something, what would it be?" Sit in the beauty parlor, on a bus, at a table in a crowded restaurant, with your ears propped open. You will have enough story material to keep you writing for a long time.

Don earns a good income, and once we were married it was no longer necessary for me to be the family provider. He expected (and I guess I did also) that once the economic pressure was off I would settle back to being what I had been once so long before, a full-time housewife.

But that didn't happen. The thing that both of us had failed to realize is that writing is addictive. It had become so much a part of my everyday life that I could no longer function without it. I got up in the morning, brushed my teeth, and sat down to confess. Story followed story, among them "My Husband Is an Abortionist" (which Don did not think at all amusing) and "One of Our Babies Must Die" (about the operation to separate our Siamese twins). This latter story brought in mail from all over the country from readers who did have Siamese twins and wanted to get information about the operation and the doctor who had performed it. It was evident even to me that I had gone too far.

"Don't you think it's time to move on a little?" Don said. "Why don't you start writing other things? How about doing some stories for the women's slick magazines, the big ones like *Good Housekeeping* and *Redbook* and *Ladies' Home Journal*?"

"I could never sell there." I told him. "I used to try every once in a while. I made one sale to *McCall's* back in my early twenties, but I was never able to repeat it. All I've received since are printed rejection slips."

"Haven't you ever had anything happen to you that would be of interest to more sophisticated readers?" Don prodded.

"Well—" A thought occurred to me. "I *did* once win a trained porpoise. We didn't keep it, but then I don't have to tell people that."

"Write about it," he urged, and, to please him, I did. "The Year I Won the Contest" was a two-page featurette. I sent it off to *Good Housekeeping*.

Back came a check for three times the amount I was used to receiving for a sixteen-page confession.

"It's a fluke!" I exclaimed. "It will never happen again." And to prove my point I wrote a story about a young bride who was homesick for her mother (myself at age nineteen) and submitted it to *McCall's*.

I received a telegram asking if $1,000 was "acceptable."

I wired back, "Yes!"

Then I sent a story to *Redbook*. It too sold.

What had happened? Why was I suddenly selling to top national magazines that had never had the slightest interest in me before? What sort of magic had occurred?

There was no magic. What had happened was that during those years spent in daily practice of my craft, I had learned to tell a story. I had learned how to compose a hook that would catch and hold a reader, how to develop characters and provide them with motivation, how to handle dialogue, how to insert "plants" at appropriate places, and, above all, how to pace a story so that it moved smoothly to a climax. Like a piano student going over and over scales, I had gone over and over the construction of a story until the elements were ingrained in my subconscious. It did not matter that the stories I had been practicing on were confessions. The things I had learned applied to the construction of all short, plotted stories. They could be transferred.

For a while I could not believe what had happened. When one story was rejected, I knew the dream had ended. "Oh, well," I thought, "I knew it couldn't last." Then, the next story I submitted was accepted and so was the one after that. I began to realize that the turndown had been no more than a particular editor not wanting a particular subject, not a rejection of my writing ability.

I continued to get occasional rejection slips. I get them today. They are part of a writer's life. But the sales were now beginning to overshadow them.

One year later a story of mine called "A Cry from the Heart" won the *Writer's Digest* Creative Writing Contest. It later sold to *Good Housekeeping* and was reprinted in five foreign languages.

It was no fluke. The lean years lay behind me.

> ... "Well—" A thought occurred to me. "I did once win a trained porpoise."
>
> "Write about it," Don urged, and, to please him, I did ...

Everyone, I think, has one year that's special, that stands apart in memory forever after. For me that year began when our rented house burned down and, the same week, the children's father—my former husband—stopped sending support checks.

We found a little apartment, and after many tries, I finally landed a job—my first. The salary was small though, and with two little girls (six and eight) and a baby of three to support, I had to find ways to earn money. I submitted "My Most Frightening Experience" to a magazine and was sealing the envelope on my entry in a "Happy Snapshot Contest" when the boom fell.

"Skita bite!" the baby said, as he came in scratching a lump on his arm. And that's how we all caught chicken pox—and I lost my job.

More job hunting—and failure. We were down to our last jar of peanut butter when word came that my "Frightening Experience" had been accepted!

"Would you like Mommy to stay home from now on?" I asked the baby.

"No," he said. He always said no. I didn't take him seriously.

Writing stories wasn't easy and they certainly didn't all sell, but the checks came in often enough to keep us going through the summer and autumn.

Then it was winter and Christmas was upon us. We got a little tree and the children decorated it with homemade paper chains. Money was scarce and I was worried.

It was then, right after Christmas, that the telephone rang and a strange, way-off-in-the-distance voice said, "Mrs. Duncan? I am happy to be able to tell you that you've won first prize in the 'Happy Snapshot Contest!' "

For a moment I couldn't imagine what he was talking about. And then I remembered—the picture of the children romping in their swimsuits.

"Good Lord!" I gasped. It would really be Christmas!

"How much?" I whispered dizzily.

"First prize, Mrs. Duncan!" the voice cried joyfully. "You have been awarded a live, trained porpoise from Marineland, Florida!"

For a long time I stood there, unmoving. Then slowly I

turned to the children who were watching me expectantly.

"Guess what?" I said numbly. "We've got a fish. A fish that does tricks."

"Don't worry, Mother." My oldest daughter came over and placed a hand on my arm. "We can eat it."

That's when I laughed. It came bubbling out of me, suddenly, amazingly, like a spring that had been untapped for too long. The children stared at me a moment, and began to laugh, too, and the wind rattled the windows and the tiny voice squeaked from the dangling receiver, trying to get me to pick it up again.

When I think back upon that awful year, that's what I remember—the laughter. For, somehow, we were making it through. And we did have a porpoise that did tricks. And even though, at the moment, it was winter, it was bound to be spring again.

("The Year I Won the Contest." *Good Housekeeping*)

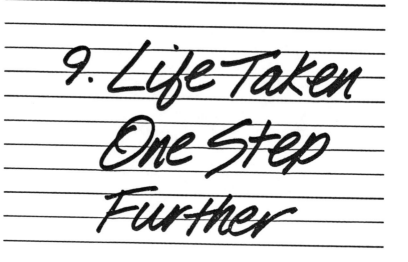

9. Life Taken One Step Further

So where did the straw come from for all those confession stories? Did I ever murder a baby? Write poison pen letters? Give birth to Siamese twins?

No, I'll admit I haven't done any of those things. But, as it was with my story about shoplifting, I know how it would feel to do them. I am sister to my confession story readers. It is only a small step between our lives.

Many children go through an irritating phase of growing that parents refer to wearily as the "why" stage. I went through an even worse one. I was a "what-iffer."

"Mother, what would you do if the house caught on fire?"

"I'd call the fire department."

"What if all the firemen had measles and their doctors wouldn't let them out of bed?"

"Why, I suppose I'd throw water on the fire myself."

"What if you turned on the water, and gasoline came out instead? What if it made the fire bigger? What would you do then?"

These conversations could go on indefinitely, and they drove my normally patient parents to the point of nervous exhaustion. Finally I was informed that I could have three what-if's a day, after which, no matter what situations I concocted, no one would answer me.

It is this same method of thinking—one which made me a totally obnoxious four-year-old—which has made it possible for me years later, as an adult, to write fiction. My own life provides the straw of reality, and the "what-if technique" makes the spinning wheel turn.

I have lain in bed, exhausted, and just as I was drifting into slumber heard the beginning whimper of a fretful baby. And heard it grow louder. And louder. And turn into a full-fledged wail and then into a demanding howl. And I've thought about that bottle of paregoric the doctor prescribed the last time the baby had diarrhea, with the accompanying warning. "Don't be concerned if your little one gets sleepy. This is a mild tranquilizer, you know." And I've thought, if ever there was a time when I wouldn't mind the baby getting sleepy, it's now.

During the months immediately after my divorce, when I was reeling with shock and hurt, I overheard two women who were supposed to be my friends commenting on my situation. "There's got to be something wrong with a woman who can't keep her husband happy," one remarked smugly. "My Tom would never dream of looking at another woman. He's got all the love he needs at home." I gritted my teeth and thought, your Tom's got girl friends all over town, honey. One of these days somebody's going to wipe that smirk off your face by telling you about them.

During the times I was pregnant with Donnie and Kate, I carried with me a nagging worry about those babies. After all, I was now an "older mother." Abnormalities did sometimes occur when women my age produced children.

The situations never went past those points. I would never give medication to a child unless it was on doctor's orders. I've heard too many horror stories about what can happen. But—*what if* I'd never heard those stories? *What if* I were very young and insecure and terrified of losing my young, selfish husband who was threatening to leave if he had to go through "one more night of this racket"?

I am the type who withdraws when hurt instead of retaliating. But *what if* my nature were different? *What if* my former friend's callousness had shoved me past an emotional cracking point? *What if* I'd written her a letter saying, "Let me tell you what good old Tom's been doing those nights you thought he was working late at the office," and signed it, "Guess who"?

Thank God, my babies were born normal. But *what if* they hadn't been? How would I have borne up?

From this thought process, fiction develops and stories form.

Let me give you the history of one of the first fiction stories I ever sold to a top women's magazine. The story was called "Lisa and the Lions." It went to *McCall's*.

The story was born one day when I was washing dishes and left my wedding ring lying on the kitchen windowsill. After the dishes were done, I looked for it and had an instant of panic before I located the ring under the edge of a dish towel.

This was the experience. No matter how entrancingly it was told, nobody could call it a short story. It did, however, set me to thinking: What if I had not been able to find the ring? I would have had to go around all day without it. People who didn't know me would have thought I was unmarried.

This was a point in my life when I was a very young mother struggling to find happiness in a marriage that I was already beginning to sense should not have taken place. How strange it would seem, I thought, after five years of married life, to suddenly find myself playing the part of a single girl again. What would I do if an attractive young man began to talk to me on a bus? What if he started asking me questions about who I was and where I lived? What would I answer?

Well, I knew what I would answer. I would tell him I was married and the mother of two little girls. That's how nice, conventional married women behaved.

But—what if I *weren't* that sort of woman? What if I were more daring, more adventurous? What if this girl—this other person I might have been—were to think, "To hell with it all—I'll just have a little fun for a few minutes." Suppose, just for a lark, she answered the question with the most ridiculous statement she could think of and said, "I'm a lion tamer"?

What if the man were emcee of a radio program and interviewed women with unusual occupations? What if he invited our heroine to be on the program? Naturally, she would refuse—or—would she? What if there was a prize given to each day's "Unusual Woman"? What if it was something she wanted and needed very much?

By the time I had gone that far, I had the makings for a story. Lisa (by now I had given her a name, for she was certainly not a "Lois") appears on the program and wins her prize. This brings forth a host of other problems. How does she explain the prize to her husband? What are the reactions of the friends and neighbors who hear the program? What if, to complicate matters further, Lisa finds to her horror that she has been selected "Unusual Woman of the Month" and is showered with publicity and awarded a trip to India? How does she keep herself from being exposed as a mere housewife? Her one little fib has grown to terrifying proportions. What can she do now?

This was my one early sale to *McCall's*. As I mentioned in the previous chapter, I was not to make another for many years. When I did enter my later, professional stage of writing, my stories were more solid and stronger and—I like to think—a good deal better. But the what-if technique was still instrumental in creating them. You cannot possibly live through every experience you want to write about, but your real-life situations can be the jumping-off point and "what if" can take you from there.

When I married Don, he was a bachelor. It was a simple thing for him to step into the family. But—what if he had been a widower with a child of his own? What if his little girl resented me for trying to take her mother's place? What if the child were so horrid to me that I could hardly bear to be around her? How would I handle things? What would I do?

The resulting story, "Bright Promise," went to *Good Housekeeping.*

I always knew I wanted a large family. I knew, too, when I married Don that I wanted to give him children of his own. Happily, I was able to. But what if I had found that I couldn't? How would this have affected our marriage? How would this sense of failure have affected me as a person? As a mother to the children I already had?

"Change of Season" was published in *Lutheran Women.*

Robin, in her early teens, in a moment of rebellion, went to a hairdresser and had her long hair cut off in a "shag." When I first saw her, I thought, "Oh, dear God, what has she done to herself!" Before long, I got used to it, and it wasn't really so bad. All the other girls of that age were getting shags too. Actually, she looked pretty cute. But that moment of initial shock stayed with me in memory. What if that long hair had symbolized something special to me about my daughter? What if she had hacked it off herself in a moment of rage? What if the result had been disastrous and she had gone into hysterics and refused to leave the house until it grew out?

"This Is My Daughter" went to *Good Housekeeping.* The girl in the story was not named "Robin" and bore no resemblance to her. I was not the mother in the story. It was not the account of anything that had really happened in our lives. But that one small, unimportant incident—the cutting of that lovely long hair—was what triggered the story idea.

If you have trouble plotting, you might try taking a commonplace situation and changing one element. Anne's husband comes home from work every night—but—*what if one evening he doesn't?* Jane lives alone in a city apartment—but—*what if she wakes one night and finds she isn't alone?* What if she hears somebody breathing in the dark next to her? Laurie always brushes her hair before she goes to bed at night. When she does this, she is used to seeing her face reflected back at her from sliding glass doors that lead to the bedroom balcony. But—*what if one evening the face reflected there does not belong to her?* In this way you will be able to give stories the authenticity that will make them ring true, and can still have the freedom to make happen—on paper—those things that never were, but might have been.

> **. . . she is used to seeing her face reflected back at her from sliding glass doors that lead to the bedroom balcony. But—what if one evening the face reflected there does not belong to her?**

Glancing across, I saw myself reflected in the glass doors that led to the balcony. The girl in the glass gazed back at me with wide, dark eyes. Her hand held a brush, half raised to her thick, black hair, and her body was slim and straight beneath the thin material of her summer pajamas. As I watched, the full mouth began to curve upward at the corners, as though this mirrored Laurie was pleased at what she saw.

It was not until I had turned off the light and climbed between the sheets that I realized what had been wrong with the picture.

The mouth on the reflected face had not been my mouth.

I had not been smiling.

(Stranger With My Face, Little, Brown/Dell)

10. High Pay Fiction

That step from the confession magazines to the women's slicks was a big one for me. The day the issue of *Good Housekeeping* containing my porpoise story was scheduled to hit the stands, I was parked in front of our corner drugstore at 8:00 a.m., waiting for the delivery truck to arrive.

It finally rolled up at midmorning, and huge piles of magazines were carried in and stacked in front of the racks. They were bound with twine.

When it became obvious that nothing was going to be done about them, I went to one of the cashiers and asked her when the bundles were going to be opened.

"Oh, we'll probably get around to that this afternoon some time," she told me. "This is one of our busy days."

I couldn't wait that long. I bought a pair of scissors and cut the twine myself. Then I sat on the floor and tore through *Good Housekeeping* until I found my story. It was back on one of the regional pages. It didn't have an illustration. But my name was on it! After all those anonymous confession stories, here at last was my name! People would read this and know that I had written it!

I bought twenty copies.

The term "women's slick" has come to mean the big, high-pay, high-prestige women's magazine that is printed on good quality (slick) paper, capable of reproducing full-color illustrations. Among the top slicks are *Good Housekeeping, Ladies' Home Journal, McCall's, Redbook, Cosmopolitan, Family Circle, and Woman's Day*. Their circulation is large, they attract high-budget advertisers, and they can afford to pay their contributors top rates. For this reason they attract good professional writers. But though the competition is tough, it's certainly not impossible. Every one of those professionals was a beginner once and had to make that initial breakthrough that led to the first sale.

"The hardest thing to find is a good storyteller," says a fiction editor at *Good Housekeeping*. "I pray for the day when across my desk there comes something that unfolds into an interesting story. What is lacking today in the short story is form. You must bring a story together; it must come full circle. You must start on a low key at the height of the action and bring that action to some definite conclusion, keeping the focus all the way.

"At *Good Housekeeping* we think that a story must have a beginning, a middle, and an end, one concretely there for the reader. I find that with most of the unsolicited manuscripts the greatest problem is the lack of this sort of form."

One main difference between the confession story and the story for the slick women's magazines is style. The editors of the slicks think of their readers as different from the readers of the confessions. They are better educated, more complicated, and less fundamental in their reactions to things. While the confession reader reacts to an insult by yelling or hitting, the slick reader bites her lip, turns away, and later weeps quietly into her pillow. But underneath the controlled exterior her emotions are strong and complex. She has dreams and ambitions. She expects a lot of herself, and therefore is often disappointed and wants constant reassurance that she is of value, not just as a wife and mother, but as a person in her own right. She is more self-contained than the earthy, spill-it-all-out confession reader; she stifles her grief, her anger, and her physical passion because she has been raised to feel that it is unladylike to "make scenes."

I find it easy to relate to this woman. She is the type who buys scissors and snips the twine from a bundle of magazines because she's embarrassed to go rushing to the drugstore manager, shrieking, "I've got to see that issue! I've got a story in there!"

The managing editor of *McCall's* describes his image of that magazine's typical reader as "a woman in her mid-to-late thirties, probably married or has-been-married, with children. We know that half of our readers work," he says, "so we think of a working situation as an acceptable ingredient in the story. We have for some time now been calling ourselves 'the magazine for the new suburban woman,' and we try to reflect a suburban lifestyle in the material we use in the magazine. What we are looking for in fiction are stories that this 'typical reader' can relate to, can learn from, or can be amused by."

The slick reader knows the difference between fact and fiction, and realizes that stories are written by professionals in order to provide entertainment and are not necessarily revelations of actual events in the narrator's life. Because of this, stories for the slicks can be written in third person as well as in first, and changes in viewpoint are permitted. The problems faced by the slick heroines are often intellectual rather than physical, and the climax at the end of the story may come with something as subtle as a shift in feeling or an understanding of something formerly uncomprehended. A simple comparison of the introductory blurbs printed beneath the titles of the stories in the confession and slick magazines makes the differences in their style and approach very clear.

"We are trying to find stories which reflect the lives and problems of our readers," the *McCall's* editor says. "For this reason, we buy a lot of our material from women writers who are writing from personal experience. We have printed stories relating to problems with children, with living arrangements for older parents, and with ways in which we can cope with the death of someone we love.

"Of course, all our stories aren't grim—we want humor, we want love stories. The important thing is that we want stories which are real and believable."

The fiction editor at *Woman's World* echoes those sentiments.

"The heroines in our stories may be single, married or divorced," she says. "The important thing is that the problems and dilemmas they face should be contemporary and realistic, handled with warmth and feeling."

The fiction editor of *Redbook* says that she, too, is looking for fiction based on reality.

"Our target reader is a young woman in her twenties who is probably married or expects to marry. Her child or children are probably preschoolers. She has had some higher education, has probably traveled and held a job that required special skills; and if she is not working now, she probably expects to return to work when her children are older. She has curiosity, a sense of humor, and a strong sense of realism.

"It follows from this that we have a special interest in stories that speak in a young voice about young-adult concerns: jobs, roommates, friends, the young-single's life; courtship, marriage, pregnancy, parenthood; money problems, housing problems, in-law problems."

In other words, all these editors want stories by writers who are willing to write about those things that are part of their own lives.

Since it is often easier to learn by seeing how something is done than by being told how it is done, let's take a look at a typical slick short story and see how it was put together.

"Heavenly Child" is a fiction story I wrote for *Good Housekeeping*. It is a short-short, which means that it is about 1,200 words—regular length stories run closer to 3,000. One's first assumption might be that this short length is easier to write, but in truth it's pretty tricky. Because it is so short, there's no room for even one word that does not further the story. Everything in a short-short has to be there for a reason.

I wrote this story deliberately because it was June and time for *Good Housekeeping* to begin buying Christmas material. Most magazines buy seasonal stories six months ahead of their publication date. This particular June, I sat out in the backyard with roses blooming along the fence and the small children in the wading pool and Kerry and a girl friend sprawled out on beach towels with suntan oil slopped all over them, and told myself, "Think Christmas. What can you do with a Christmas theme that hasn't been done a hundred times before?"

The idea that finally came to me was inspired by friends of ours, Lou and Molly, whose family of six children included two who were adopted Korean orphans. Molly had once described to me these children's arrival:

"We were stunned. We had expected cute little cuddly babies, not these poor, miserable little creatures. Their arms and legs were like match sticks, and they had distended bellies and huge, haunted eyes. They could have been ads for CARE packages."

The children are teenagers now, healthy and beautiful. I had often thought of the love and patience that must have gone into making them that way. Was there, I wondered now, some way in which I could use this subject and incorporate Christmas at the same time? How could I tie the two together?

I managed, and the resulting story was published not only once but twice, for two years after it first appeared it was re-run with a change—the child in the story was no longer Korean but Vietnamese. In italics preceding the story there was an editorial comment: "Because this story is more timely today than when it first appeared in *Good Housekeeping*, we are reprinting it to remind our readers of other orphans in need and of the spirit of another Child who had no place to rest His head."

The tiny parking lot behind the Happy Hours Kindergarten was already filled but they found a space across the street. Even from there they could hear the children singing carols loudly.

"Well, it's noisier than it was in September," Molly said,

trying to laugh. "Remember how sort of strained it was then, meeting all those parents and children for the first time? And Kim so quiet—"

"She sure wasn't quiet tonight," Louis said as they got out of the car. "The whole time I was driving her over she never stopped chattering about the picture she's going to show us and the fact that she got picked to come early to help mix the punch. She's made great adjustment, honey. Don't forget, these are the first children she's really had a chance to know."

"And the first complete families," Molly added, "ones she could relate to." Their own friends were mostly the parents of teenagers. She and Lou had waited a long time before they accepted the fact that there would be no child of their own, longer still before they had seriously considered adoption.

When they had made their decision . . .

Does this construction look familiar? It should. We've started with a hook right before the main action of the story; we've set the scene and introduced the main characters (Lou, Molly, and—still off-stage—Kim); we've presented a problem (Molly's concern about Kim's being able to relate to people unlike herself); and we've gone into our flashback to show how things got to be as they now are:

As we go into the flashback we find Molly's mother questioning their decision to adopt a Korean baby and Molly explaining that they want to share their lives with a child who really needs them.

"You're asking for problems," her mother had said worriedly. "Granted, there is nothing cuter than an Oriental baby, but when he gets older and compares his family to others, will he ever really feel he belongs?"

"Of course," Molly had cried, thrusting the warning from her. But had she, she wondered now, disposed of it too quickly? Would it come back to haunt her on this peaceful night of the children's party?

Kim had defied them right from the start by not being a "cute Oriental baby . . ."

I now get to use Molly's description of what her babies had

looked like upon their arrival in the States. From here we move chronologically forward, carrying Kim through babyhood, through her first words—"Mama" and "Dada" and "Nana."

> By the time Kim was four she had become a definite personality, funny, endearing and stubborn. She had also developed a strong feeling about her own identity. "I am Kim Jordan," she would say in a tone that invited no argument. "My daddy is Louis Jordan. My mommy is Molly Jordan. My grandma is Nana Jordan."
> "No. Grandma is Nana Elliot," Molly would correct her. "She has a different name from ours."
> But Kim would not accept this. "No," she would state firmly. "We are all in one family, all the same."

Each step of the flashback is used to accentuate the problem that Molly is worried about—Kim's possible crack-up when she realizes how different she looks from the rest of the family. Molly and Louis go through the adoption story, and Kim won't listen. "That's a dumb story," she says, "tell something else." And so Louis tells the Three Bears, and, listening, Molly thinks how much little brown bears look like big brown bears and how vulnerable her child is:

> She mustn't be hurt, Molly had thought fiercely. She musn't ever be hurt. And at the same time the question had risen unbidden within her: Did we do the right thing? Will she thank us later? Or will the time come when she looks at us and sees us not as parents but as members of an alien race with white skin and round eyes?

So they enter Kim in kindergarten—with Molly continuing to worry—and we see Kim's apparent adjustment there. And now we come out of the flashback at exactly the place where we entered it, with Molly and Louis getting out of the car to attend the Christmas party:

As they crossed the snowy lawn the noise grew louder, and when they went in it poured upon them in a wave of festivity. The big front room was ablaze with color, paper streamers of red and green draped the ceiling, and a tall tree glowed with rainbow lights. In the center a long table held platters of cookies and a shimmering punch bowl.

People were everywhere—mothers, fathers, grandparents—but the kindergartners themselves were the stars. They rushed about, chirping like happy sparrows, as they dragged adults by the hand, pointing out paintings and projects, giggling and squealing and bubbling with joy.

Kim was standing motionless beside the punch bowl. When she saw Louis and Molly her face came to life. Handing the ladle to the girl beside her, she worked her way toward them.

"Did you see my picture?" she asked.

"Not yet," Molly said. "Where is it?"

"There on the wall."

Here is where we utilize our "plants," come full circle, and tie the beginning of the story to the ending. Louis drove Kim to the party early (he had to, because if she had been in the car with her parents they couldn't have talked about her on the way over and the reader wouldn't know the situation) so that she could "help mix the punch." Now, here she is by the punch bowl, one thing echoing another. As he drove her over, Louis said, "She never stopped chattering about the picture she's going to show us." With this statement, the fact of the picture was "planted" in the reader's mind. When Kim brings it up now, the reader doesn't ask, "What picture?" She already knows. She's been *expecting* a picture. Every word of the short conversation that took place between Molly and Louis in the car was put there for a reason, so that now, at its end, the story will come together into a satisfying whole.

And now, the climax at which point the problem is solved:

Turning, Molly saw that the far wall was covered with children's drawings. Two dozen proud Josephs guarded two dozen gentle Marys, and two dozen mangers tilted precariously in as many directions. Angels perched daringly on rooftops, and a varied assortment of lopsided stars gleamed on high.

"Which is yours?" Molly asked, and even as she spoke she felt her husband's arm go around her. His other hand dropped to rest on his daughter's glossy black head.

Then she saw it—the picture of the blond Joseph bent protectively over his blond Mary. From the manger, on a mound of hay so high that any less perfect babe would have rolled off onto the stable floor, a raven-haired, almond-eyed Baby beamed up at His parents.

This sort of construction works well for the short-short story, where the general rule is that the onstage action takes place in a single day and preferably within a few hours. By using the flashback technique, we can confine the actual story to this restricted time limit while working all the necessary background material into the flashback. In "Heavenly Child" the onstage action takes about ten minutes—it starts when Louis and Molly park their car and ends with their encounter with Kim inside the nursery building—but by using the flashback we are able to bring in all the information about Kim's past which is needed in order to make the incident with the picture significant.

What sort of stories are the editors of the women's slicks looking for? Well, let's start with the things they *aren't* looking for. Here are some types of stories that are extremely difficult to sell:

1. *Stories that are not laid in the present.* Historical novels are very much "in"; surprisingly, however, historical short stories are seldom used in magazines.

The exception may be the juvenile magazines where such stories are considered educational.

2. *Stories written from the viewpoint of a child.* Editors receive many of these and occasionally use one, but only occasionally and only if it is exceptional. You have a far better chance of selling your story, even if a child plays a prominent part in it, if you write from the viewpoint of one of the adult characters.

3. *Stories written from the viewpoint of the very old.* These tend to be depressing. It is difficult, too, for the average reader to relate to elderly protagonists. It's true that all of us are going to be in that boat someday, but most of us would just as soon not dwell upon the fact. On the other hand, we can fly back easily in our minds and hearts to the time when we were nineteen or twenty. It seems like yesterday, and always will.

As with stories written from a child's viewpoint, editors will buy an occasional extremely good one, but your chances for a sale are greatly increased if you tell your tale from another angle.

4. *Stories about offensive subjects*—sex deviation and blood-and-guts murder—or stories using vile and obscene language. Realistic as such things may be, the woman reader gets enough of them from other sources. She does not relish them in her recreational reading.

5. *Slice of life or "literary" short stories that build to no definite conclusion.* The slice-of-life, as its name implies, is a little section of life plucked out of context and presented for the reader's observation. She looks at it and responds with some sort of emotion—"Oh dear, isn't that terrible!" or "How strange and lonely this makes me feel!" or "How true! How true! That's just the way a person like that would act!"

Slice-of-life stories, like abstract paintings, are usually either very good or very bad. Many of our literary classics are slice-of-lifes. Sad to say, however, there is little demand for them in today's market. Most editors now tell us they are looking for plotted stories that are carefully constructed so that they move forward, and between the beginning and the end something is accomplished.

The women's slicks offer the highest pay for magazine fiction. How might the experiences of your life be slanted so they may find a home there?

. . . A simple comparison of the introductory blurbs printed beneath the titles of the stories in the confession and slick magazines makes the differences in their style and approach very clear . . .

"I Carried That Dreadful Disease—
My Husband Must Never Know"
I remembered—oh, so well—the rapture of our love at first when even the slightest touching of our hands brought a leaping desire. But now I didn't dare to let him touch me, and, even worse, I couldn't tell him why!

(*Personal Romances*)

"What the Heart Decides"
Anne was a sensible girl with her feet on the ground. Then why was she flying away from the man she loved?

(*Good Housekeeping*)

"We're to Blame If Our Baby Dies"
Why doesn't she wake up...why doesn't our baby move! We only gave her the pills to make her sleep, to stop the crying. Oh, God, help us, please!

(*True Secrets*)

"A Second Baby Is Different"
If you, like Sally, wonder why a second baby is different, we suggest that you read this story.

(*Chatelaine*)

"My First Husband's Kisses"
Could I ever learn to love this man I'd married—cherishing the bittersweet memory of my first husband's kisses?

(*Modern Romances*)

"From This Day Forward"
Once she had been in love madly; this time she wanted to be much wiser.

(*Good Housekeeping*)

"I Made My Son a Daughter"
He was my child—but no longer a child! Now he was lost and frightened in torture I could only imagine. And even though I had made him the way he was, I couldn't undo the damage now!

(*Personal Romances*)

"Bright Promise"
I loved this child; I loved her father. Surely we could all have a life full of warmth and happiness. But, somehow, I had done something terribly, terribly wrong.

(*Good Housekeeping*)

"One of My Babies Must Die"
They're such tiny mites, each fighting so hard to live, each so precious to me! Yet I must make the decision that will take one of them from me, and I keep asking myself: How can I do it? How *can* I?

(*True Confessions*)

"Home to Mother"
She adored her baby. She loved her husband. But she didn't really like being a wife, and Rick knew it.

(*McCall's*)

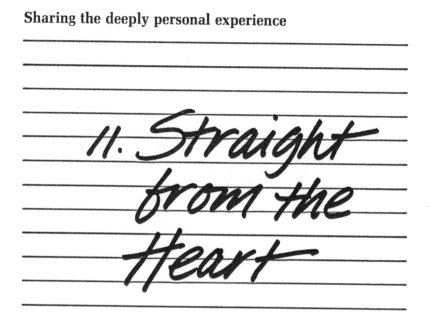

11. Straight from the Heart

Every writer has, somewhere in his file or desk or scrapbook, a favorite story. It may be "favorite" for any number of reasons. Perhaps it represents the first major sale or has achieved popular success or has taken a national award. Perhaps someone whom the writer respects has selected it for favorable comment. Perhaps it was a particular joy to write, falling onto the paper so easily that it seemed almost to create itself.

But, most likely, the favorite story has meaning because it came out of the depths of the writer's heart.

So far in this book, I have discussed the techniques of professional writing. These are important, because, just as a builder needs to know how to anticipate stresses on framework and foundations, the writer must know how to assemble words and arrange them in such a way that an article or a story doesn't fall apart.

But the design of a cathedral takes more than knowledge of how to use hammer and nails, and a story that will be remembered by the reader long after the book or magazine has been closed must be more than a collection of carefully arranged sentences.

The full-time professional writer does a lot of work that comes from the head alone. The resulting creations are known as "potboilers," because they bring in the necessary regular income that keeps food on the table. There is nothing wrong with writing a good potboiler; in fact, it is necessary to be able to write one if writing is the way in which you earn your living.

Yet every once in a while, if we are lucky, that special story will happen—the one that comes singing out of the heart. It cannot occur constantly, for who among us has that much heart to give? When it does come, it is like a gift, something that has been created through us rather than by us.

In my own case, such stories have been few. In this chapter I am going to discuss one of them. "A Cry from the Heart" (not its original title, but one bestowed upon it by an editor) was written after the death of my mother. Much of it is autobiographical; some of it is not.

Psychologists tell us that one of the strongest emotions experienced by a person who has lost a loved one through death is guilt—guilt for not having done more, for not having expressed more, for ever having been irritable or petty or neglectful. The overwhelming knowledge that time has run out and there is no longer an opportunity to do or undo anything is so horrifying that it overshadows all the good memories of happy times. In this story, I set as my heroine's goal the acceptance of the fact that the love between her and her mother had been so strong that the small frictions had not truly mattered. As an obstacle, I placed the daughter's painful and guilty memory of her own unpleasantness.

The story was therapeutic for me to write, enabling me to come to terms with my own feelings. I wrote it, too, for my father, brother, and aunt, whose grief was as deep as my own. Later, when I could view it more objectively, I realized that it was a well-written story, and I sent it out into the world with the thought that it might hold meaning for somebody else. I was amazed to find the response so immediate and so strong. I received letters from people all over the country saying, "This is my story. How did you know?" Somehow, without even meaning to, I seem to have touched a universal nerve.

Somehow I know it, and yet, I don't.

I stand here in the living room, running the vacuum, and my eyes keep turning to the slot in the door through which the mail will be falling at any time now, and I am waiting for the envelope that will not be there. A slim, blue envelope with a familiar, lilting handwriting, as distinctive as a voice—

"Honey, how's it all going? What did Robin finally select to play for her solo? Enclosed is a recipe for a seafood thing I tried last night on the Werners. Successfully! Just don't let it brown too long. Have you had a chance to read the new Agatha Christie? Not her best, of course, but still—" **(1).** (See page 139)

I have been back home for over two weeks now. It was exactly a month ago today that the phone rang and my father's strange, controlled voice said, "Lois, a terrible thing has happened. Your mother has had a heart attack." **(2.)**

I was able to get a flight to Florida that night. Don did not go with me; somebody had to stay here with the children. I did take the baby, who was only three months old and still nursing. I sat on that plane, staring out the window at the blackness of the sky, and I thought, my mother is dying—my mother—my mother. But it was not true, I knew. My mother, only 57 years old, her hair barely touched with gray, her eyes flashing bright, incredible blue, her laugh, that gay, right-out-of-her laugh—**(3.)**

"Honey," she said only weeks ago, "honey, you nut-nut, what do you mean, am I tired? Why should I be tired when you're the one who's just had a baby?" **(4.)**

There was some mistake, of course. A flu bug, maybe. It could hit people like that, making them seem so sick so quickly, or if it was a heart attack, people recovered from those. You read about it all the time, people going on for years and years, taking care of themselves, babying themselves a little.

When I got there she was dead.

My mother.

My father met the plane. I saw him waiting there behind the glass window and there was no one beside him, no red coat beside him. He held out his arms. I could see that through the glass, but when I came inside he only said, "Is that really the baby? I thought he would be bigger. In the snapshots your mother brought home with her, he looked so big." He said, "How are you? Was it a smooth flight?" My young, handsome, arm-around-everybody father, suddenly a million years old, his eyes fixed somewhere past me on a spot on the wall.

My brother got home a few hours later. He flew in from California with his new bride. Daddy and I had gone to bed; we could not sit up and talk. Somehow, we could not talk to each other at all. We were both in bed, though neither of us was asleep, and the door flew open, for neither of us had thought to lock it, and my brother and his wife were there, crying. "Hello! Hello! We're here! We were able to get an earlier flight than we planned on." Then, after we had all hugged and kissed, there was a silence.

Bill, my brother, said, "Was it fast?"

Daddy said, "We were just sitting there reading the mail. There were letters from you both, you and your sister. We were laughing about Robin—" (my eldest daughter)—"Lois sent us the program from the orchestra recital, and Robin's violin solo was the same piece your mother had played in her first recital. Such a funny coincidence, and we were laughing—" **(5.)**

His voice broke. He turned and left.

"How could you?" I asked my brother, and he said, "But Lois, we have to know, don't we?" And we glared at each other, the way we used to when we were children, picking back and forth at each other because we were late for naps.

"I'm sorry," I said. "You're right, of course; we do have to know."

Bill said, "I shouldn't have asked right off like that," and he and Carolyn went into the guest room, and I lay back down on the sofa, which was where I was to sleep, and we finished the long night.

There was a crib set up there in the living room for the baby. My aunt had somehow located it and had it delivered—how I still don't know, but it was waiting there when I walked through the door. The baby slept noisily, snorting, snoring, making restless infant sounds, and I lay there listening, wishing I had left him at home with the others. The house was all about me from my childhood, and Mother was all about the house.

There was a picture hanging on the bedroom wall, a child's sloppy watercolor of a woman with blobs of blue for eyes and a funny, lopsided, grinning face. It was a Mother's Day portrait that I had painted in the third grade. **(6.)**

"Mother," I had wailed when I gave it to her, "I meant so to make you beautiful!"

She had looked at the portrait and then at me, and her face had crinkled into laughter. "Oh, honey," she had said, hugging me, "oh, you silly nut-nut, don't you think I know that?" **(7.)**

Framed, the portrait still hung in the bedroom where my father slept, or tried to sleep, and next to it was my wedding picture, the one from my second wedding, for she had ripped up that first one. ("Good riddance," she had said.) That first marriage had been when I was 18, so determined that I was grown and wise.

"Mother," I had cried, "can't you understand that we're in love? Don't you remember what it was like? Haven't you ever loved anybody?" I said such dreadful things that day, all self-righteous and clever and spiteful. "You just don't want to let me go," I told her. "You can't stand the thought of an empty nest. You don't want me to be happier than you are."

Dear God, I really said that. I said that.

When the marriage ended, I came home. I walked in the door with three small children and my father said, "I'll kill that irresponsible . . ." and Mother said, "Yes, let's." She came over and took the baby out of my arms—the old baby who is now my big boy, my big six-year-old—and said, "Let's all have a drink. And then we must eat something; we must try to eat." It was *we*, not *you*. "We must just start over," my mother said as we choked down our dinner.

I stayed there for five long months, doing nothing. Thinking back now, I can see that I was like a person who has had a long illness, limp and unthinking and unfeeling, content simply to be. I did not even look very often at the children.

At last, one day, Mother said, "This has gone on long enough now. It is time to pick up the pieces. Where do you think you would like to live?"

I looked across at her. She was sitting in the big chair by the window, with the baby in her lap and the two little girls at her feet doing a jigsaw puzzle. It was like a picture with the lamplight falling on them, and the woman with the blue eyes and the three children, a unit in themselves with myself sitting away from them, watching. **(8.)**

"To live?" I said. "Why, here, I suppose. Where else?"

"Not here," Mother said. "Daddy and I have raised our fam-

ily. We have so many plans for the next years, I just don't see
how we can start over again with a houseful of youngsters.
Here, I think this one is wet right now." She got up and
brought the baby to me and plunked him down into my lap.

"What about New Mexico?" she said. "That's a nice place.
Your brother's stationed out there and could introduce you
around. You could probably get a job at the Air Force base, and
there would be a nursery there for the children. Have you kept
up with your typing? Do you think you could pass the Civil
Service exams?"

I stared at her, not believing I was hearing correctly.

"You don't want us here?" I said.

"It's not that, honey," Mother told me. "It's just that—well,
Daddy and I have been planning this trip. It's not a sudden
thing; we've been thinking about it for a long time. As soon as
you and Bill were grown and we had our freedom, we were going to take three whole months, just the two of us, and really
travel. See the country. Maybe dip down into Mexico."

"And we're keeping you from it?" I asked.

"Well, it would be easier to leave if we knew you were set-
tled somewhere. New Mexico is such a lovely state, and with
Bill there to help you get started—"

"And rid you of the responsibility." My voice came out in a
kind of rasp. "Don't you worry," I said harshly. "You can be
free. I won't hold you down a minute longer. I wouldn't stay
here if you paid me to. If you think I need you to lean on,
you've got another think coming."

That night I phoned my brother, and the next week the children and I left for New Mexico and a new life—and, eventually, Don.

Oh, Mother and I patched things up. She and Daddy were
out to see us at Christmas. As far as I know, that's the only trip
they took, despite all their planning. I came back to Florida on
vacations, and the summer that Don and I were married my
parents took the children so that we could have a honeymoon
and find a house large enough for the five of us.

When I flew to Florida to collect the children, they were
brown and glowing, wild and gay and noisy but so big, suddenly. Mother said, "I'd forgotten how many three children
could be!" They had gone swimming every day and fishing,
and they had read together all the books from my childhood
years.

"Did you know," Mother said, "that Robin loves poetry? She has almost memorized the whole of 'The Chinese Nightingale'!"

" 'And spring came on forever!' " Robin quoted proudly. She threw her arms around her grandmother's neck. "Oh, La-la, I don't want to go. Can't you come with us?" **(9.)**

"Oh, we'll be visiting soon," Mother said. "We'll have dozens of Christmases and summers."

But we were invited to spend that next Christmas with another family at Aspen. It was such a wonderful opportunity for the children to learn to ski, and my parents understood perfectly. And that summer we simply had to go to Michigan to see Don's family, because here I was, already pregnant with their next grandchild, and they had never even met me or the children. We would, we swore, go to Florida the next summer for certain. Nothing, absolutely nothing, would keep us away—

My father had waited for me to arrive before choosing a coffin. **(10.)**

"I thought you would know which one," he said, my father who never waited for anyone. "I thought you should pick."

So we walked through that place, Daddy and Bill and I, and there were thirty-eight different models of caskets. I counted them.

"That one?"asked Daddy, pointing to a wall. He could not look.

"No," I said. "This one here." A slim, gray box without satin inside, without a foam-rubber mattress, without carvings.

"She hated the expense of funerals," I said. "We read that book, the one about the cost of dying in America, and she said 'Honey, don't ever throw good money into a fancy casket for me.' And she wouldn't want flowers either. She would think that was so wasteful—all kinds of lovely flowers when she couldn't even smell them." **(11.)**

Mother!

That night for the first time I was left alone in the house. A friend had invited the whole family for dinner, but I had chosen to stay home with the baby, who must have his feedings, so I was alone there except for Don Jr., in his crib, and I walked through the house and called out loud, almost screaming it, "Mother! Mother!" There was a recurring nightmare I used to have when I was little of waking and calling and no one coming. It never ever happened that I can remember. Always when I woke, Mother was there beside me, soft and warm and smelling of sleep, but I still kept dreaming it. I was in that nightmare now, back to three years old again, calling, "Mother!" No one answered. This time the nightmare was real

The next day was the funeral. We almost missed it. The babysitter did not arrive, and Daddy, Bill and Carolyn and I were stuck there at the house with the official limousine waiting for us out front and the baby howling in his bed. Finally my aunt found an ex-cleaning woman of hers, who came rushing in, and we got to the church and there was the gray box that I had selected, and dear God, Mother was in it. **Mother was in it!**

I must have gasped, because my aunt reached over to steady me. My father put his hand over mine, and my brother, on the other side, put his hand to cover ours. All our hands clutched each other as that ghastly box went up the aisle, and I shut my eyes and kept trying to think: Soon I will be home with Don, picking up the kids' toys and scrambling eggs and running the vacuum—

As I am doing now. Over and over in the same spot. The mail finally arrives. It falls through the slot, as I have been expecting, and lands in a spattered heap. I drop the vacuum. I hurry to it and, of course, there is no blue envelope, but there is a note from my father—**(12.)**

"Everyone is kind," he writes. "The Kantors had me for dinner last night, and tonight I am going to the MacDonalds'. There have been so many contributions to Project Hope in your mother's name."

He writes, "The place is so empty. I think I do not need such a big place. Your aunt has been staying here with me, but still, it is too big."

He writes, "I think perhaps I shall take a trip. A little trip. Somewhere."

I pick up the vacuum again. The roar is strangely steadying.

My daughter comes in. She is the eldest, Robin. She is thin and tall, almost as tall as I am. She has long, light hair and brown eyes and my mother's sharp, straight nose, and she stands next to me and says, "Mama?" **(13.)**

"Yes," and I turn off the vacuum, for something is wrong.

"Mama," she says, "I'm so awful. I did something so awful. Mama, I can't stand it, I just can't." Robin who never cries, the one of them all who never cries, throws herself upon me, and I take her in my arms, this child, who is almost my height, who cannot even get her face down into my shoulder.

"Mama," she cries, "I keep thinking and I can't stand it, I was so terrible!"

"What?" I ask. "What are you talking about?"

"To Lala. That time that we stayed with her and Grampa, that last time when you and Dad were on your honeymoon, remember? Remember?"

"Yes."

"I told her I hated her!"

"What?" I start so that the child in my arms jumps too, and wails, "Mama, I did, I did. She said to make my bed, and I didn't want to. The others were watching cartoons, and hadn't made *their* beds, just left them all sloppy under the spreads, and why should I have to be the one, just because I was oldest—and I said—I said—"

"Yes," I say, holding her close.

"I said, 'I hate you, Lala! You're mean!' " The terrible words are out. She goes into a shuddering siege of weeping. "Oh, Mama, you don't think she thought I meant it, do you? I didn't! I didn't ever mean it!"

"Of course not," I say, so quickly, so certainly. "How could you?"

I hold her through the storm.

"Oh, honey," I say, "for goodness sake, don't be such a nut. You know how Lala felt about you. You were her grandchild, her very first, the one who read poetry, who played the violin. You were her joy, her absolute joy!"

"But, I *said*—"

"Honey," I say, "do you think that could have mattered to her?"

And in my silent soul I scream—out—out—past my daughter—past the silent vacuum cleaner—and the windows—and the skies—and the clouds—and whatever goes past that into the great, incredible, unbelievable forever—

Mother, Mother—I cry—I love you I love you I love you!

And back it comes, softly, sweetly, full of that familiar, laughing grace—

Why, honey, don't you think I know that? Why, you silly nut-nut, don't you really think I know that? **(14.)**

That, then, is my favorite story, written in an outpouring of grief and love and memory. Yet, it did not simply pour itself, uncontrolled, upon the page. By the time I wrote this, I had been writing stories for so many years that certain basic techniques of storytelling had become ingrained. I used them automatically to create the effect I was trying to achieve.

Let's go back and look at what some of them were:

1. The introductory paragraphs are used to set the stage. There is nothing here that is not important to the story that will follow. The mother's letter establishes the intimacy of the relationship between mother and daughter; this isn't the sort of letter people write when they correspond twice a year. It's the chitchatty note of one who writes frequently. Mother and daughter exchange recipes and compare their reactions to books; it's almost like a continuing conversation.

Another important thing we do here is introduce Robin. Robin is going to trigger the story's climax, so we must "plant" her existence early. Notice, too, that Robin is the only one of the three older children who is referred to by name. The others are simply "the children." They are props in the story, not actual participants in advancing the action, so we don't clutter the story line by making them true personalities.

2. Flashback. We know all about those, right? But in this case I'm experimenting with tenses by changing from present tense into past. Sometimes this sort of thing works, and sometimes it comes off sounding artificial and strained.

3. Token description. When working in short fiction, it is impossible to give full descriptions of the characters. It would simply use up too many of your allotment of words. One way to get around this problem is by choosing a couple of physical features or character traits that are particularly representative of the person you want to describe. Present these to the reader and let him build his mental picture around them.

In the case of my mother, I have chosen her blue eyes and

her warm, rich laugh. At various times during the rest of the story, when I want a picture of Mother to leap into the reader's mind, I refer again to the blue eyes and laugh, and let his own thought processes do the rest.

4. Symbol. The term "nut-nut," used as an endearment, is going to symbolize the loving closeness between the two women. I am "planting" it early.

5. A reference to Robin again. I don't want the reader to forget her, as she has an important part to play. I also want to accentuate the closeness of Robin and her grandmother, via their joint interest in the violin, as this relationship is going to parallel the relationship between the mother and grown daughter.

6. Now we are going to move into a flashback within a flashback. Have you found in your own writing that there are often problems getting into and out of flashbacks? Here is one simple method of doing this; it's the use of a "transition vehicle." A transition vehicle is something that is in the present and was also there at the time of the flashback, and you sort of ride back on top of it. In this case, it is the watercolor painting. Notice how easily it takes us back in time.

7. This is one of the most important sections of the story, as it foreshadows the climax. When the reader reaches the final scene, he will think back to this and understand its significance.

8. Blue eyes again, our token descriptive feature.

9. Again, we tie Robin and her grandmother close. They read poetry together. And the poem they are discussing is significant, for the line Robin quotes is, "And spring came on forever," which foreshadows the meaning of the story—that love is never lost.

10. Back out of the flashback. There's no easy, gently sliding transition this time, but an abrupt jump as the startling reality of the caskets jolts the narrator.

11. Again, we plant the closeness between mother and daughter. They not only read books together and discussed them, they discussed such things as death and each other's last wishes.

12. Out of the other flashback and into present tense.

13. I decided to have Robin call her own mother "Mama," as "Mother" has come to mean the narrator's mother and we don't want confusion.

14. The symbolic endearment at the story's end.

Why did I write this story? Quite simply, because I had to. I wrote it for myself first and for others second. I submitted it for publication because I wanted it to be read so that my mother would come alive for others. By living on, via the printed page, she seemed, somehow, to have gained a measure of immortality.

It is one of the deep satisfactions of being a writer, that one can do this—create immortality for others. And perhaps, by so doing, we also in a way create immortality for ourselves.

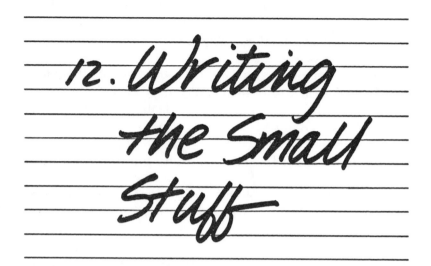

12. Writing the Small Stuff

One of the nicest things about a writing career is that it can be expanded or compressed to fill whatever time is available at various stages of your life. During those years when you are going to school, working at a full-time job, or raising a family, that time may be at a premium.

There are writers I know who set their alarms for 5:00 a.m. in order to put in a couple of hours at the typewriter before leaving for work. There are others who leave the dinner table and write until midnight. One of my students worked the night shift as an attendant at the airport parking lot; he said he got a lot of writing done during those quiet hours right before dawn. Another did his writing only on weekends. He had converted the attic of his home into an office, which he reached by climbing a rope ladder and entering through a trapdoor. Then he hauled up the ladder, turned on the air conditioner to drown out the noises from below, and worked until dinner time. His wife didn't like that very much; she kept worrying about what would happen if the house caught fire and there was no way of letting him know.

The housewife-writer may seem to have things easier. After all, she's sitting home all day anyway, isn't she? With to-day's labor-saving devices, housework shouldn't take up more than a couple of hours. She can write all the rest of the day if she wants to.

Which does sound reasonable—except that it just doesn't work that way. During the years when there are babies to rock and toddlers to chase, free time is limited; when children are sick, company is coming to dinner, or costumes have to be made for a school play, it may not exist at all.

Then, suddenly, there may be a slice of time handed to you unexpectedly, like a present. You stand there clutching it, asking yourself, "What can I do with it?" You cannot bear to waste it. It's too precious. There's not enough of it to do some-thing big with, but you *have* to use it.

You go to the typewriter and roll in paper, and your mind goes blank. You know that if the time were greater, or if only it was more dependable—if you could count on its occurring in some regular manner—you could tackle a major project like an article or a story. But at this particular point, time just doesn't come like that. Even now as you sit there staring at the white emptiness of the paper before you, your little piece of time is going, going. The phone rings. Or a child calls. Or your secretary knocks on your door to announce there's a cli-ent in the waiting room. And it's gone.

If your life is like this at the moment, it's helpful to have a list of small writing projects that you can draw upon, things that do not take huge hunks of unbroken time but can be worked on in odd moments.

Let me list a few of these that you might want to consider:

Column Contributions. Many magazines have columns that are based upon reader contributions. The highest paying of these is *Reader's Digest*, which uses 300-word anecdotes "revelatory of adult human nature and providing appealing or humorous sidelights on the American scene" for their col-umn "Life in These United States." Breaking into this col-umn isn't easy (an editor once informed me that the maga-zine receives more than 5,000 anecdote submissions a week and that they are assigned "by the pound" to editors for review) but there are others for which the competition is not as heavy. *Guideposts* has a section called "Quiet People" for which they buy short features of 250 to 720 words. *Family Circle* wants material for their "Woman's World" page. *Good Housekeeping* wants material for their "Better Way" page. The various mothering magazines want personal experiences to which other mothers can relate.

Perhaps the largest markets for column material are the confession magazines. *True Experience* pays $200 for stories for their "Dreams That Really Come True" column. *True Love* has a column called "How I Know I'm in Love," and *Modern Romances* has one called "Family Traditions."

These stories do not all have to be sensational. I once sold an anecdote to *True Story* for their "Women Are Wonderful" column about the time Robin, Kerry, and a friend of theirs formed a singing trio that performed for club programs and at dance intermissions. There was nothing unusual about the subject matter, but I ended on an inspirational note: "We watch them, even we their parents, and we find ourselves being drawn with their audience into a time we had almost forgotten—when the world was made to be conquered, when nothing was impossible, when fame and glory shone directly ahead on a still untraveled road."

Letters from Readers. Many magazines pay $5, $10, or as much as $25 for letters from readers who have suggestions to offer about how to do something better or more easily. Such suggestions may be in the form of recipes, accounts of how you solved a particular problem, or helpful hints about such things as baby care, money management, saving electricity, planning meatless meals, or simplification of household chores.

Woman's Day has a column called "Neighbors," and pays for each letter printed there. *Baby Care* wants letters for their "Family Corner." *Parents* buys letters that contain anecdotes "illustrative of parental problem solving with children and teenagers" for the "Family Clinic."

If you enjoy letter writing, you need not confine yourself to family and friends. Add some magazine editors to your list, and make that daily trip to the mailbox really worth your while.

Contests. I have been a contest nut since the age of eight when I submitted my first entry. It was a poetry contest, and the poem (I remember it still from first verse to last) was about a shipwreck. It began:

> 'Twas a million miles or more
> From the nearest glimpse of shore.
> The captain lay upon the deck.
> His head was full of gore.

It won a prize. Why, I cannot say. Perhaps it was the happy chance that "shore" and "gore" did rhyme, and there was "more" thrown in there for good measure. Whatever the reason, my entry brought me a Captain Midnight sweatshirt and a fanatical love of contests. I have been entering ever since and have won some extraordinary prizes (remember the porpoise?).

There are contests for everything imaginable: slogans, verse, essays, song lyrics, jokes, recipes, product descriptions, names for newborn zoo animals. There are so many people in the world who cannot write a complete sentence that those of us who can stand an excellent chance of placing in competitions that require written entries. For those who take their contest-entering seriously, there are contest newsletters that will keep you informed about everything going.

Verse. You will notice that I do not say "poetry." The demand for serious poetry of the kind you have to study to understand is practically nonexistent in paying markets. Poetry finds its place in poetry journals and literary magazines, which add to the author's reputation in academic circles but almost never bring in any money.

But for rhymed verse, there *is* a market. Most of the religious publications use inspirational verse; the juvenile magazines print a great deal of it; and some of the high pay women's slicks run several short poems per issue. Payment runs from a high of $5 per line (*Good Housekeeping*) to 25 cents per line (some of the Sunday-school publications). You will never get rich writing verse, but there are many personal experiences that can be captured better in a few carefully chosen words than in a full-length story or article.

Greeting Card Verse. If you are really into verse writing, you might want to look into writing greeting card verse. Most card manufacturers buy freelance material and pay somewhere between 50 cents and $3 a line for conventional verse, and from $10 to $55 each for humorous or studio cards.

The biggest buying season for Christmas verse is midsummer, while winter is the best time for submitting spring verse for Valentine's Day, Easter, and Mother's Day cards. Birthday, anniversary, and get-well greetings are in demand all year around.

The best way to learn the ins and outs of this kind of writing is to browse through the greeting card racks the next time you are at a drugstore or card shop. Notice who publishes the cards you examine and how they differ from one another.

While some companies publish all types of cards, others deal exclusively in sweet and sentimental greetings. Many companies specialize in studio cards, while still others go in for the cute or "soft touch" variety. Some manufacture cards with gimmicks attached or with tricks and puzzles. Others feature inspirational and religious motifs.

Greeting card verses are short, seldom more than eight lines and often only four. The usual pattern is for the second and fourth lines to rhyme, with the first and third lines unrhymed. Occasionally you will find greetings written in couplets (first and second lines rhyming, third and fourth lines rhyming, etc,). There is also a growing market for unrhymed greetings—short, simple, well-worded messages of caring.

The key word when writing greeting cards is "sincerity." Remember always that the person who buys the card you write does so because he wants to express a particular sentiment and is either embarrassed or unable to come up with the right words to do so on his own. The words are yours, but the thought is universal. If the language of your verse is stilted and too formal, or overemotional and mushy, your buyer will pass it by and look further for wording that makes him feel more comfortable. Think about those people in your own life you care deeply about. How do you express your feelings for them? Let the words come naturally, from the heart, and the message will ring true for others as well.

Verses are usually submitted on separate, typed, 3x5 cards. Center the verse and put your name and address at the top left corner. Always number your verses and keep copies, so that if a company writes and says, "We are buying #17," you will know which verse has been sold.

Mail your verses out in lots of no fewer than ten and preferably no more than fifteen. Less than ten seems skimpy and is hardly worth the postage, while more than fifteen may be overwhelming to an editor. If you send too many verses at once you will be competing with yourself. If there is a special sort of illustration that you think should accompany your verse, make a note of the suggestion on the card; otherwise the choice of artwork should be left to the editor. Art is seldom purchased from freelancers, but is assigned to members of the staff.

With your verses, you will, of course, enclose a self-addressed stamped envelope for their return if they are not purchased.

Devotionals. Particularly in demand by the religious magazines is the brief, uplifting piece known as the "devotional."

Madge Harrah, a well-known religious writer who has contributed hundreds of devotionals to *Guideposts*, outlines the format as follows:

1. Begin with a quote from the Bible, a hymn, Shakespeare, etc. This quote must pertain to the anecdote which is to follow.

2. Describe an experience that you or someone you know has had. The anecdote must be short and make one definite point.

3. Draw a conclusion that gives the reader an inspirational message to carry away with her (the typical reader of devotionals is a woman).

4. End with a prayer. It need not be more than one sentence long.

"For a devotional, you must think small," Madge advises. "Don't try to deliver a full-fledged sermon. You don't have the space for that. Your goal for this sort of piece is to take your reader *one step* closer to a better life or deeper faith in God."

An example (this devotional of mine was purchased by *Guideposts*):

"Every one that asketh receiveth" Matthew, VII, **7**

My 9-year-old daughter and I were jumping waves in the Gulf of Mexico when Kate said, "Mother, I can't touch!" I grabbed her hand to pull her toward me and realized suddenly that I couldn't either.

I'm a competent swimmer, so I was not overly worried.

"Hang on to my shoulders," I said to Kate, "and I'll tow you in."

But I was figuring without the undertow. No matter how hard I swam, we remained in the same spot. All around us other vacationers were laughing and romping in the water, and I felt embarrassed for them to see my helplessness. I knew that if I could manage to move only a few feet closer to the shore, I would be able to touch bottom.

Fifteen minutes later, I had to face the truth. The current was too strong for me. Incredible as it might seem, right there a couple of yards off a public beach, Kate and I were going to drown.

"Help!" I cried. "Help!" People turned to stare, apparently thinking I was playing some sort of game. Then Kate, catching my panic, began to scream also. A tall young man strode out from shore and easily drew us to safety.

Why is it so difficult for some of us to swallow our pride and admit that we have gotten ourselves out too far and cannot plant our feet on solid ground?

Lord, help us, please, to overcome our reluctance to appear "weak" or "silly." Give us the sense to know when it is time to turn for help to others—and to You.

How-To Projects. Detailed instructions for things to do or make are sought by many magazines, especially juveniles. If you are good at handicraft projects and have workable, original ideas about how to make a Halloween mask out of aluminum foil, or Christmas tree ornaments out of frozen orange juice containers, you may well have found your place in life. These projects should be simple enough for a child to complete on his own or with a minimum amount of help from a teacher or parent. Especially in demand are projects that relate to holidays.

There are also entire magazines devoted to crafts at the adult level. These run from every conceivable kind of sewing project to furniture building and room decorating. The trick here is to be able to compress your instructions into the tightest possible form, while still keeping them easy to follow. I had one student who financed a do-it-yourself garage-into-rec-room project by writing up and photographing each step of the transformation.

If you can supply photographs along with your instructions, you will have a greater chance for sales. Magazines usually prefer to receive 8x10 black-and-white prints on glossy paper. If you live in a town large enough to sell film, it probably contains a photo lab that does custom printing. When you deliver your roll of exposed film there, they will develop it for you and make you a contact sheet, which consists of tiny prints made from your negatives, all on one sheet of paper. You can look these over, compare angles and exposures, and select the best frames to be enlarged. If you decide to try color, you should be sure that your film is the type used for slides, not prints, as magazines like to make their reproductions from positive transparencies.

A word of caution—when writing a how-to, don't take the intelligence of your readers for granted. Be sure to cover each step of the how-to process, no matter how obvious it might seem, and be careful about your wording. One writer I know sold a large circulation women's magazine a recipe in which she instructed readers to "heat one can of mushroom soup." An incredible number of people rushed to do exactly that and placed unopened cans of soup directly on heated burners. The cans, of course, exploded, causing countless injuries. Both the writer and the magazine were bombarded with law suits.

Fillers. When juggling ads and text, it's seldom that an editor can come out exactly even. There is usually some empty space left over at the bottom of some pages. The short pieces editors use to plug up these gaps are called "fillers," and they can consist of almost anything. Religious magazines often use original prayers and inspirational thoughts and meditations. Other publications use jokes, and household tips. One of my students sold an animal publication a one-paragraph anecdote about how she and her husband handled their two jealous dogs.

These writing projects may seem insignificant in comparison with full-length articles, stories, and novels. It is doubtful that you will want to spend your life writing in any of these areas (though there are people who do). My main reason for including them here is that so many people with real talent allow their creativity to dry up completely during their lives' high-pressure years. I have seen this happen often. A promising woman writer will marry, produce children, and find herself caught up in what my student Mary Johnson described in her *Home Life* article as the "demand, response; demand, response" syndrome. Frustrated by the constant demands upon her time and energy, she makes a conscious or subconscious decision to postpone her writing efforts "until a better time." Men do the same thing; "When things ease up at work—When Johnny's no longer in Little League—When we move to an apartment and there's less yard work to do—

When I retire," they tell themselves, "then I'll write."

The problem is that talent, unused, is also undeveloped. The bright mind, unchallenged, forgets how to be creative. Small writing projects, scattered through the days, are like sitting-up exercises done regularly every morning. They may not be the same as cross-country ski trips or ten-mile jogs or championship games of tennis, but they do help to keep you from becoming flabby. Later, when there is opportunity for the big stuff, you'll be in good enough shape to handle it.

. . . there are many personal experiences that can be captured better in a few carefully chosen words than in a full-length story or article. . . .

CHRISTMAS, PRESENT

I saw the Ghost-of-Christmas Past
Glide by our lighted tree.
Her arms were filled with dolls and toys.
And all were meant for me.
I sensed the rustle of her skirts.
Her blouse was trimmed with lace,
And when she turned to smile at me
She wore my mother's face.

Just as this vision slipped from sight
I heard my daughter call.
Wild footsteps clattered on the stair;
Shrill giggles filled the hall.
She burst into the gift-filled room
And squealed in glad surprise,
And all the Christmases-to-Come
Were mirrored in her eyes.

How swiftly fly the rainbow years,
Like splintered shafts of light,
As fragile as the gentle ghosts
Who whisper in the night.
I draw my child into my arms
And hold this moment fast
Against the time my face will be
Her Ghost-of-Christmas-Past.

(*Woman's Day*)

13. Writing the Big Stuff

I wrote my first book when I was twenty-two.

It didn't start as a book, but as a short story which I titled "The Presentation Ball." The idea for the plot came to me one day when I was thumbing through my hometown paper and found on the society page a schedule of events for the "debutante season." I went back and read it again, for I couldn't believe my eyes. A *debutante season*, in a little town like Sarasota, Florida? A town whose one high school had such a small student body that everybody ran together regardless of background? The most popular students and class leaders during my high school years had been the children of people from all walks of life—doctors, fishermen, orange pickers, lawyers, insurance adjusters, the tightrope walkers from the Ringling Brothers Circus. Things could not possibly have changed so much in such a short time.

What a gruesome holiday season, I thought, for a girl whose friends were all awhirl in the high school scene but who could not, herself, make the debutante list. What a painful situation. And what a good story idea.

I worked hard on that story, and I was pleased with it when

it was completed. I decided as I wrote to have my heroine, Lynn, forbidden to participate in the debutante season because her idealistic father did not feel it was democratic. Lynn, who has always been a member of the "best crowd," resents being forced out of it. When her steady boyfriend is drafted to escort a girl whose mother is organizing the ball, her resentment increases. The story builds to the Presentation Ball, when a series of events helps Lynn to regain her sense of values.

The story did not sell. I was completely bewildered. The situation was interesting and the characters believable. Still, back it came from one magazine after another, even good old standby *Seventeen*, which had been publishing my work regularly.

In their case, a letter accompanied the manuscript.

"This is good material," the editor wrote, "but it is not right for a short story. There is too much to it for that. There is more than one girl's story here; it is the story of a whole town. Have you considered making this a book?"

Had I considered writing a book? Of course I had. It was a dream for some distant day when I was more experienced. The thing that scared me about the thought of a book was the simple fact of its size. A short story might run up to fifteen pages or so, while a book would be more than 200. How many years would it take to write one, and how could I help but get bogged down along the way? Write a book? I wasn't ready yet! It was too big a project to attempt. I would work up to it gradually by continuing to turn out stories for teen publications, where I was comfortable. Then, perhaps, someday when these became too easy, I would be ready for a staggering endeavor like writing a novel.

Still, here was an editor who should know what he was talking about, and he was telling me that I had book material. Besides, I had a head start. "The Presentation Ball" was seventeen pages long. If I cut it in half, I could call it two chapters. Then, if I tacked five chapters on to the beginning and five on to the end, I would have a twelve-chapter book.

Such were my thoughts as I got out a new box of paper, put

Robin (age two) and Kerry (six months) down for their naps, and set up my typewriter on the kitchen table. Such were not my thoughts six weeks later when I read over the chapters I had written and dropped them into the wastebasket. It took me that long to realize that what I was attempting was not going to work. Writing a novel by adding on to a short story was just about as sensible as trying to make an evening gown by adding taffeta to the top and bottom of a swimsuit.

There was little I could add to either the beginning or end of "The Presentation Ball" that would have any bearing on the story, which was centered around a girl's personal reaction to a difficult social situation. Anything that happened before that point in Lynn's life (her childhood, grammar school experiences, summer trips with her family) or afterward (college, a job, a husband and babies) was superfluous.

The confines of my story were set. I could not make it longer, only larger. To do this I had to enlarge on the theme itself. The short story had a "plot," a string of related events leading to a single climax. For a book, I had to go deeper; there would have to be a series of climaxes, each furthering the story and leading Lynn a little further along the road to maturity. Instead of a simple plot, a book must have a theme, and the one I decided upon was this: "A year of difficult social change, although at first deeply resented, opens a young girl's eyes to ways of life other than her own and helps her mature into a better person." Since the Presentation Ball was only one incident in the development of the theme, I changed the name of the novel to *Debutante Hill*.

I knew now what it was I was trying to prove; my next problem was how to prove it. How could Lynn's difficult year change her radically as an individual? To work this out, I asked myself some questions: If Lynn can't take part in the social activities she is used to, what does she do with her time? Does she sit home and brood? Does she make friends with girls who have not been selected for the debutante list? What kind of girls will these be? How do they react to Lynn, whom they must regard as a bit of a snob? What is Lynn's reaction when her steady is drafted to escort a deb to the parties? Does she retaliate in some way? If so, how? Does she attach herself, perhaps, to another boy, one she knows her parents won't approve of?

When I reached this point I was so interested in what was going to happen next that I could hardly bear to leave the typewriter to walk out for the mail. That was when I knew the story was truly under way.

When you are working on a book-length project, the organization of your material is important. When writing short stories, I had produced the first draft at one sitting or at the most two, going back later to revise and polish. With a book, of course, this technique was impossible, and I found myself losing my train of thought between work sessions. This was a time in my life when I was able to work without interruption only during the little girls' naptimes, and in order to remember exactly where in the story I was, I would spend half that precious time reading through the previous chapter. Then, often, I could not remember what I had planned to have happen next. By the time I finally got things worked out so that I was ready to start putting words on paper, the bedroom door would pop open and there would be Robin, all slept out and ready to go to the beach.

So I was forced to begin using something I had avoided for years—an outline. I made one for each chapter, a thin but complete framework of action and dialogue, so that I needed only to glance back over one page to see what I'd done in the previous chapter and to glance one page ahead to see where I was going in the next one.

It took me four months writing two hours a day to turn "The Presentation Ball" into *Debutante Hill*. As I stood finally with my impressively bulky manuscript in my hands, I realized with amazement that I had never enjoyed writing so much. I had been afraid to try writing a book; I had expected it to be a kind of endurance test with all the difficulties of short story writing magnified many times over. It had not been that at all. In fact, it had been the easiest kind of writing I had ever attempted.

This must sound absurd to people who have not experienced the contrast. Why should it be easier to tackle a 60,000-word project than a 3,500-word one? Perhaps to some it wouldn't be, but in my own case the toughest part of writing is the planning—selecting the right experience for my jumping-off point, constructing the plot, and organizing the material. Once this is done, the writing itself is fun. Working on something book length was a relief because I no longer had the strain of having to keep coming up with new short story plots and having to drop good characters I was really starting to like in order to pick up new ones. The pleasure of a book is that once you get it outlined you are set for months and can relax and enjoy the flow.

You can also enjoy your characters. In a short story you must make every sentence count. The limited wordage means a precise structure, built carefully on a framework of plot from which nothing must be allowed to detract. Your characters are restricted in their actions and dialogue to showing only those parts of themselves that move the plot forward.

A book may be more loosely constructed—there's breathing room; and since it has a broader theme, the more fully developed your characters are, the better. You have room to make them well rounded, to get their viewpoints on things, to listen to their casual conversations. You have freedom to look into their hearts and show not only the characteristics that bear directly on the plot, but also those that make them interesting as human beings.

In "The Presentation Ball" I had had Lynn's father, Nathan Chambers, tell her simply, "No, you may not be part of this debutante thing. It's ridiculous." In *Debutante Hill* I was able to present this man in depth so that the reader could know the "why" behind his attitude—his own problems as a struggling young intern in love with one of Atlanta's most popular debs, leading to an elopement which caused great bitterness between Lynn's mother and her family.

Another character who appeared briefly and insignificantly in the short story was Lynn's sister Dodie. The reader was told only that Lynn and Dodie had little in common and did not get along. In the book there was room to develop Dodie as a person, to see her in rivalry with her sister, to hear their arguments, to study their contrasting reactions to a variety of situations. As Lynn matures during the course of the year, we see the two girls beginning to grow closer. Lynn's gradual acceptance of her sister becomes a mark of her own change of character. Even though it is a subplot, it furthers the main theme.

Debutante Hill was published by Dodd, Mead & Company in the fall of 1958 and won the Seventeenth Summer Literary Award. I have never understood its success. When I look back upon it now, in the light of the sophisticated literature that is being written for young people today, it seems simplistic and amateurish. I cringe a little at the stiffness of the style, and wonder that I ever had the nerve to send it into the market at all.

The thing I did have going for me was my closeness to the material. I was a contemporary of Lynn and her friends. I knew how their minds worked. I knew the town in which they lived and the school they attended. I had lived in that town and attended that school. I knew what the cafeteria smelled like and how the lockers sounded when they clanged open and slammed shut, and what girls whispered about in the dressing room after gym and how teachers looked at you when you held hands with your boyfriend in the hall. We had not had debutantes when I attended Sarasota High School—but it was not difficult to take that extra step—to say to myself, "What if . . .?"

The publication of my first book was an ego trip. I'll never forget the pride I felt that year when I went down to renew my driver's license and listed my occupation as "author" rather than "housewife."

I won't try to describe my book-writing career in detail; suffice to say that once it started it kept on going. My early books, like *Debutante Hill*, were sticky-sweet romances. Then, in 1968, I wrote my first young adult adventure novel. Dodd, Mead refused to publish it ("It's not your style of writing. We want your *love* stories") but Doubleday was willing to take a chance on it. *Ransom*, which is still in print, was runner-up for the Mystery Writers of America's "Edgar Allan Poe Award," and suddenly librarians, who hadn't known before that I existed, began to take notice of me.

Ransom was followed by more adventure stories and mysteries for teenagers; a couple of adult novels which were not too successful; a historical novel; a biography (a disaster); and some books for small children. In 1971, I wrote *A Gift Of Magic*, a landmark book for me because it was the first novel of mine that had to do with psychic phenomena and the supernatural. It was rejected by Doubleday ("It's not your style of writing. We want your *mysteries*")—and by six other publishers as well before it was finally accepted by Little, Brown. The book was well received and established me as a forerunner in a genre that has since become hugely popular.

Another special book for me was *Summer of Fear*, because it was my introduction to the crazy world of film-making. That book, also published by Little, Brown, was about an Albuquerque family (very much like my own) that was being intimidated by witchcraft. Retitled "Stranger in Our House," it was televised as an NBC Movie of the Week, starring Linda Blair.

Kerry, who at that time was living in Hollywood, trying to break into motion pictures, auditioned and won a small part in the movie. She called me often to tell me what was happening.

"You know the little dog Trickle in the book?" she asked me.

"Of course, I know him," I said. "After all, I created him."

"You wouldn't recognize him now," said Kerry. "Linda Blair likes horses, so Trickle is now a horse."

My mind flew immediately to the scene in which the witch put a spell on Trickle and killed him, and Rachel, my heroine, buried him under a rose bush. I could picture the carcass of a horse (would the name be changed to "Gusher?" I wondered) rotting in the scorching New Mexico sun while sturdy little Linda shoveled away, day after day, at a trench.

I need not have concerned myself. That scene was eliminated from the movie, along with almost everything else that made any sense. All the scenes I had placed around an Albuquerque swimming pool were staged at a California riding stable, and the handsome lifeguard Rachel was in love with was transformed into her riding instructor.

Near the end of the filming, Brett and I flew out to spend a few days with Kerry, and she took us to visit the set.

"Rachel," she said to Linda Blair, who by this time had taken on the persona of the character I had created, "I'd like you to meet my mother, Lois Duncan. She's the one who wrote the book."

"Rachel" regarded me blankly.

"Oh—was there a *book*?" she asked in amazement.

I realized then how God must feel about atheists.

That movie, bad as it was, was very good publicity. Today I'm the author of more than thirty books, the majority of them young adult suspense novels which hinge (in a "what if" way) upon personal experience. I've also written an autobiographical how-to, *Chapters: My Growth As a Writer*, which was named a "Notable Children's Trade Book in the Field of Social Studies."

I think back fondly on *Debutante Hill*, that old-fashioned thing with all its imperfections. It was one of the most important writing projects I ever undertook. Having written that book, I realized that I could write others. From then on I knew where it was I wanted to go.

> **. . . in the light of the sophisticated literature that is being written for young people today it seems simplistic and amateurish. I cringe a little at the stiffness of the style . . .**

There was something about Lynn Chambers, a fineness of bone, an ease of bearing, a graceful, unconscious little lift of the head, that made newcomers to Rivertown, who had never seen her before, nod approvingly and ask, "Who is that?"

And whichever long-time resident was asked would usually know.

"That's the older Chambers girl," he would say. "Nathan Chambers' daughter. You know Dr. Chambers—they live on the Hill."

"Oh, yes, of course."

Even if someone did not know of Dr. Chambers, everyone in Rivertown knew about the Hill. The Hill Road ran at an easy slope down to the river, and along it lived the society families of Rivertown. . . .

(*Debutante Hill,* Dodd, Mead, 1957)

He could not get air into his lungs; he could not move his limbs. The terrible fear froze him and deadened his senses. The silence was gone now, and the night was filled with voices—a chirp, a growl, a twitter—a burst of high-pitched laughter. How could he have thought that the clearing was empty! It was alive with frenzied movement, as the faceless shapes milled about him, crazed creatures from some evil other universe.

(*Daughters of Eve,* Little, Brown, 1979)

14. Team Writing

So, if it's so satisfying to write "the big stuff," why don't more people do it?

The answer is simple. They are scared off by the same thing I was—the seeming immensity of the project.

Just ask a few, and you'll get similar answers.

"It would take so long! I'd never get finished!"

"Writing is such lonely work. I can't imagine sitting by myself at a typewriter day after day without any human contact."

"I'd never have the self-discipline to keep myself working, to set my own deadlines and meet them without outside prodding."

It's an indisputable fact that writing a book is an awesome undertaking. The mere idea of a 200 to 300 page project can be pretty overwhelming, and the challenge is more than many people are self-confident enough to be willing to tackle completely on their own.

That's how it was with the members of a writing seminar I taught one summer. It was a great class of talented students, many of whom mentioned during the course of the semester that they would like to write novels "but will probably never get around to it."

The last day of class, a woman named Marion Woolf got to her feet.

"Look," she said, "a chapter is only about ten pages long. If a person wrote only one page a day, he'd have a chapter done in a little over a week. There are enough of us in this class so that if we each wrote a chapter, we'd have enough wordage for a book. How about it? Shall we give it a try?"

The idea was greeted with enthusiasm, and when class was over, twelve students impulsively signed up to collaborate with Marion. By the first group meeting, four had reconsidered and changed their minds. The rest remained undaunted. Even if each had to write *two and a half* chapters, they reassured themselves, the book could still be completed within a month.

It didn't take long, however, for them to begin to realize that the project would not be as easy as they had expected.

Their first idea had been that the book would be a "modular" novel—a series of separate events, each constituting a chapter, which could be constructed separately and then lined up in almost any order. They also visualized each chapter as being written from the viewpoint of a different character to allow for the variety in the authors' writing styles. Soon, though, it became obvious that if they did this the effect would be disjointed and the book would lack a feeling of cohesiveness. What they needed, they came to realize, was a strong plot to hold the segments of the story together and provide a conclusion toward which to build.

The plot, they created by brainstorming.

"We used the 'question-and-answer' technique," explains one writer, Margery Papich. "We decided to lay our story in our hometown of Albuquerque, since it was a locale we were all familiar with. Then, since our city is the site of the annual International Hot Air Balloon Fiesta, we thought it would be fun to center the action around a balloon kidnapping. The whole thing seemed so exciting and colorful—a political

highjacking in front of thousands of unsuspecting specta-
tors! Once we got that far, the questions and answers came
automatically. Who would commit the kidnapping, bad guys
or good guys? We decided on good guys. Why would nice
people do such a thing? We had to think a while before we
had an answer for that. Maybe, we decided finally, they were
staging a protest. What would nonviolent, law-abiding citizens feels so strongly about that they would protest in this
manner? An unfair tax, perhaps. But what sort of tax would
be outlandish enough to drive gentle people to stage a Southwestern version of the Boston Tea Party?"

Layne Torkelson, whose husband was a solar engineer, offered a suggestion. What about a tax on the sunshine used for
solar heating?

As their story began to take solid shape in their minds, the
group assigned themselves popular adventure novels to read
so they could analyze how such books were structured. They
then created a "time line" by outlining the story chronologically on a blackboard in a way that provided them with a
skeleton. During the course of more brainstorming sessions,
they revised this outline, altering sequences of events and
filling in details. When this was completed to their satisfaction, they finished blocking out the book by dividing it into
chapters.

As might have been expected, when the project began to
prove more complicated than they had anticipated, a number of formerly enthusiastic participants began to fall by the
wayside. Some didn't contribute their fair share of work and
were dropped by default. Two people moved out of the state,
and one decided that she didn't like team writing and would
prefer to write a book of her own.

At this point, the remaining members of the group decided
it would be wise to hire a lawyer to draw up a joint venture
agreement so there would be no misunderstanding about
how the profits would be shared if the book was accepted for
publication. It was decided that everyone who had attended
the first meeting would receive a token payment, but that the
largest portion of the profits would be divided among those

who continued to participate until the book was completed.

By the end of the summer, the number of aspiring authors involved in the project had been reduced to only three—Marion, Margery and Layne. It was time now for the actual writing to begin. They divided up the scenes, set deadlines for themselves, and sat down at their individual typewriters. Each wrote in the seclusion of her own home, but they met often to coordinate their efforts and to review and edit one another's work.

"We passed pages around so constantly that all three of us ended up writing and rewriting every chapter," says Layne. "For better or for worse, we eventually even adopted the same writing style. We became so involved in each other's work that when the book was finished we couldn't remember which of us had written what sections of it."

The last step of the writing process was the polishing. This consisted of nine full days during which the three authors read the manuscript aloud to one another. This "read through" revealed to them the areas in which further work was needed. The women rewrote and revised, trimming down scenes that ran too long and lengthening those that seemed too skimpy. They smoothed transitions, found substitutes for overused adverbs and adjectives, and edited for consistency of style. By the time they had their final draft typed up and ready for submission, the "quickie" book that they had originally expected to toss out in just over a week had taken them fourteen months.

Group writing with three or more people involved is unusual. Two-person writing teams are far more common, and, not surprisingly, many of these are composed of husbands and wives.

There seems to be no one "right way" for writers to work together. When I asked three teams of author-friends what their own particular process was, I received three different answers:

1. Aimee Duvall and her husband, David Thurlo, a teacher at a junior high school, write historical romances. Aimee does the research and writes the first drafts, but she leaves "holes" for David to fill in when he gets home at night.

"I'm good at dialogue and emotional scenes, but David's better at description," she says. "When I'm rolling along and come to a spot where I need to have something described, I'll leave David a note to 'describe Jessica' or 'insert a description of the hotel room.' He also critiques each day's output and makes suggestions in the margins for changes for me to make in the final draft."

2. Angel Milan and her husband, Ted Lynn, collaborate on romances also. In their case, however, although they brainstorm together, Ted is the "idea man."

"He does a large amount of the plotting," Angel says. "He has a knack for pinpointing the weak spots and coming up with solutions."

Angel does 99 percent of the actual writing; then Ted goes over the manuscript and edits and proofreads.

3. Michaela Karni and Sue Bernell, two close neighbors, write mysteries together under the pen name "Karin Berne." These good friends share all phases of the creative process equally, writing alternating chapters and serving as each other's editor.

"We feel team writing beats solo writing hands down," says Sue. "Neither Michaela nor I was able to get published on our own, but since we started working together we've sold five novels."

My former students had a productive partnership also, although they spent one discouraging year mailing their manuscript off to publishers and getting it back. Finally, after six rejections, their tenacity was rewarded, and they received the phone call that they had been hoping for.

"Your book is charming!" said an editor at Dodd, Mead and Company. "We love it and want to buy it."

Since they had met in my seminar and it was there that they had conceived the idea of a team writing project, the authors decided to publish their novel under the name "Duncan Tres" ("three from Duncan's class.") I was thrilled. Their editor, however, was not. She thought "Duncan Tres" was a dreadful name and, at her insistence, the byline was changed to "Marion Margery Layne," a combination of the first names of all three authors.

Whether my name was on the cover or not, I was proud and delighted to consider myself "Godmother" to *The Balloon Affair*.

. . . the remaining members of the group decided it would be wise to hire a lawyer to draw up a joint venture agreement so there would be no misunderstanding about how the profits would be shared . . .

JOINT VENTURE AGREEMENT

We, the undersigned, agree that we join in the venture of the writing of a book tentatively called *The Balloon Affair*. We agree that we shall bear the expenses of this venture equally and share any possible first sale profits in this manner: Marion Woolf, coordinator, will receive two shares; contributing writers will receive one share apiece.

Writers are considered contributing when they meet deadlines with acceptable material for the book. Deadlines and acceptability of the material will be determined by the coordinator, Marion Woolf. Writers submitting material judged unacceptable will be given two opportunities to revise the material to make it usable for the book. If the writer fails to submit acceptable material after two revisions, within a deadline set by the coordinator, the writer will be considered noncontributing.

In the event the book is published, noncontributing writers will be paid a flat fee of $75 for total compensation for any idea or ideas they may have contributed to the project.

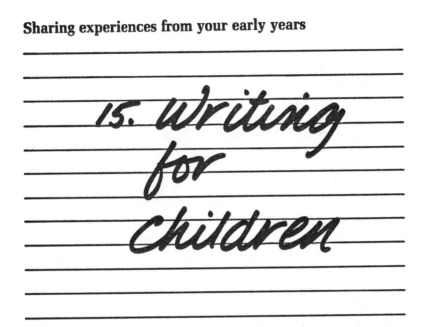

15. Writing for children

One day when Robin was three and Kerry was one, I opened the refrigerator and found a toy fire engine inside. It had been "one of those days." I'd been up at dawn with Kerry, whose normal rising time was 5:00 a.m.; the washing machine had overflowed; the dog had diarrhea; and we were having company for dinner. Somehow in my frantic surge of house-cleaning before guests arrived, I had stuck the fire engine in the refrigerator instead of in the toy box.

Robin thought this was the funniest thing that had ever happened. For days afterward she carried the tale around the neighborhood, announcing to everyone she saw, "I've got a silly mother! She does dumb, dumb things! She is so silly, silly, silly!" Then she would double over in a fit of giggles.

My mind made its usual clicking sound.

If it's all that funny, I thought, I might as well write about it.

Silly Mother was my first book for small children. It was the story of a little boy who worries about his absent-minded mother. Not only does she put his fire engine in the refrigerator, she puts his pajamas in the puppy basket and the puppy in the pajama drawer. In the end he is brought to realize that the poor woman hasn't really gone round the bend, she is simply exhausted, and if he picked up his own mess and gave her a little help around the place she might be able to get it all together.

My neighbor, Suzanne Larsen, offered to do the illustrations. Suzanne's hobby was painting, and with her own youngsters and mine to use as models, she thought it would be fun and easy to put together a children's picture book.

Suzanne and I laid out the book with babies climbing on our backs and crawling around between our feet. I had just acquired an agent, and we sent the book to her to market for us. Incredibly, it was accepted by Dial Press. It was then that we discovered exactly what it was we had gotten into.

First there was the matter of the number of pages. Books, we discovered, are printed and paged in multiples of eight: sixteen pages, thirty-two pages, forty-eight pages, etc., never anything in between. Suzanne and I had arbitrarily decided that forty-two would be a nice number and had planned the illustrations accordingly. Now we learned this was impossible. The whole layout had to be scrapped.

We had also assumed without question that the pictures would be in full color. That dream went down the drain fast. Each color used increases the printing cost. A book with full-color illustrations costs a mint to produce, and unless the author has a name that will guarantee sales, the publisher is almost sure to lose money. As a comparative unknown, I was worth no more than two colors. Out went Suzanne's beautiful paintings.

The editor wrote that he wanted the overlays done on dinobase.

"Overlays? Dinobase?" Suzanne responded blankly.

Dinobase overlays turned out to be clear sheets of acetate which were placed over the basic black and white sketch, and the areas that would later be in color were inked in. There was a different overlay for each color, and everything had to be lined up to fit perfectly. I, who had thought the whole procedure was to draw pictures and mail them off, watched in helpless sympathy as Suzanne, who had thought the same thing, ransacked the library and ran from one commercial artist to another for help and information.

The book was a fluke. It was a Junior Literary Guild selection, and Suzanne, after this self-inflicted cram course, went on to become a professional artist. The whole situation, as I think back on it, was beyond belief. We had no right to produce a successful book that way, but somehow we did, and that experience was my introduction to writing for children.

The field of juvenile writing is a rich one for the personal experience writer. Each one of us has a childhood to draw upon. Those of us who are parents have our children's childhoods as well. In my own writing, I find myself laying my stories in Florida beach towns like the one in which I grew up, and peopling them with characters who resemble my children and their friends.

Mary Calhoun, author of the popular Katie John books, wrote the first of those because she was homesick for the big old house she had lived in as a child.

"So, I brought it back again, and put Katie John in it," she says. "Readers ask me, 'Is Katie John you?' No, she isn't—she's the child I always wished I could have been. I was a dreamer, while Katie is a doer. She rides the dumbwaiter down into the walls of the house, when I didn't dare try because the pulley ropes were old and tattered.

"Yet some of Katie's problems and most of her emotions are ones I experienced as a girl. Others are those I observed later in my own children and their friends. There was a time, for instance, when my young neighbor, Daphne, was going through the eleven-year-old blues. I flew back in time, and all those old feelings rose within me, just as they had been when I was eleven. These are the things I write about—how it feels to have a fight with your best friend; what you do when you feel put down by the 'in' kids; how you feel when you really want some event to happen. Anger, hurt, eagerness—these are universal emotions. They don't change from one generation's childhood to another."

There are commercial advantages to writing books for children. The main one is that they seem to go on forever. *Mary Poppins* was published in 1939. *Doctor Doolittle* in 1922, and *Heidi* in 1880. *Little Women*, which our Kerry reads even today, to have her annual cry, was published in 1868 and continues to sell year after year in undiminished numbers. While the adult novel seems either to go off like a skyrocket or plunk to earth like a dud, the average juvenile sells in a steady, consistent manner, bringing in its unspectacular but always welcome royalties, for an indefinite length of time.

Why this pattern of selling? Well, for one thing, children rip books up and the libraries have to keep replacing them. It may be years before an adult novel needs replacement, and by that time it is usually out of print. A children's book, however, becomes crayon-marked, frayed, and peanut-butter-smeared so quickly that librarians have to constantly reorder it just to keep it on the shelves.

There is also a turnover in readership, as one set of youngsters outgrows a book and younger brothers and sisters move up to take their places. A parent who has seen a book loved by one child will buy it for a second when he reaches the appropriate age.

The juvenile book field can be best considered as three separate age groups:

The Preschool Picture Book. If you have decided to try your hand at a juvenile, this is probably the area that will come immediately to mind as the best place to start. You will think, as I did, how simple! It's hardly longer than a grocery list. I'll just toss off a few hundred words with a moral at the end and get Suzy-down-the-street to whip up some cute pictures to go with it, and there we'll be!

As Suzy and I discovered, there's a good deal more to it than that. One problem for the writer is that with this type book the pictures are actually more important than the writing. The Caldecott Award, which is given annually for the year's best juvenile, is presented not to the author but to the artist. Often a picture will cover a whole page with only a line or so of text running opposite. The royalties for such a book are usually split equally between the writer and the illustrator. With this the situation, you can imagine that illustrators often prefer to write their own stories. This doubles the competition for new writers.

Still, there are success stories—many of them—*Silly Mother* being an example. When writing the text for a small-child's picture book, the writer must think in terms of scenes. People cannot simply sit in one room and talk to each other. There must be enough action going on and enough variety of background so that the illustrations will not become monotonous.

There was a time when stories for this age group were all fairytales filled with talking animals and elves and witches. No more. An amazing amount of rich and meaningful material turns up these days in the form of juvenile literature.

Some examples: Drawing upon her own childhood memories of life with a hearing impaired sister, Jeanne Whitehouse Peterson wrote *I Have a Sister—My Sister Is Deaf*, a sensitive, child's-eye-view of what it is like to be an older sister to a handicapped child.

Her second book, *That Is That*, the story of a family deserted by the father, was based upon feelings Jeanne experienced herself at age ten when her father died, leaving her, her mother, and her younger sister alone.

"When you write for children, you must peel back to the core of childhood like you peel back an onion," she says.

The painful honesty of Jeanne's books has been both lauded and criticized by the parents of young readers.

"*That Is That* had only been out a month when I received my first hate letter," she recalls. "It was from a mother who thought it was terrible to suggest the possibility that parents aren't forever. The thing is, though, they're *not* always 'forever,' however much we might wish that to be the case. The knowledge that life can go on, even with a parent gone, is an important thing for a child to have."

Jeannette Caines' book, *Daddy*, also is the story of a child of separated parents (Jeannette's close friends) who sees her father only on Saturday. Another book, *Abby*, about an adopted child, was inspired by Jeannette's experiences with her own adopted daughter, and Lunchbox, about three little girls who take turns pairing up as "best friends," is about that daughter and her love-hate relationship with two cronies.

Jeannette, who grew up in Harlem, writes for and about black children.

"Part of my life is in every one of my books," she says.

Another author, Ruth Luhrs, writes for Navajo children. Her books are published on the Navajo reservation by the Navajo Curriculum Development and Production Center and used as textbooks in the schools there.

"Mine is a specialized kind of writing," Ruth says. "Someone who doesn't have an intimate knowledge of Navajo culture would have a hard time doing it."

Both women feel that there is a great need for books about the experiences of minority children.

An offshoot of the preschool picture book, for which there is an increasing demand, is the easy-read book. While the preschool book is read to children, the easy-read is one that the child in early grades can read himself. There are standard vocabulary lists which can be obtained by writing to publishers. The need is particularly strong for easy-read books for boys. Nine out of every ten learning-disabled children are male, and it is not uncommon to find a boy who is doing fine in every other way but is reading far below his age level. This youngster needs an easy vocabulary, but he wants to read about characters his own age with whom he can identify, and he wants them to be doing exciting things.

I recall my own frustration as I went from store to store trying to find appropriate books for my learning-disabled child during grammar school days. Everything was either too babyish in subject matter or had too difficult a vocabulary.

The Book for the Middle-Aged Child. The eight to twelve-year-old group represents the Golden Age of Reading. The deadly D's (driving, drinking, dating and drugs) have not yet impinged upon the time of the Golden Ager, and librarians tell me they can't keep enough books on the shelves to satisfy him.

Think back to yourself at this age, and you will have no trouble finding subjects to write about. These children are interested in everything. This is the animal-lover stage. What pets did you have as a child? How did you feel about them? This is an age for exploring and mystery, for secret clubhouses and hideouts away from grownups' prying eyes. Did you have such a place? Of course, you did. Mine was the hollow in the center of a clump of bamboo. I would sit in there for hours at a time for the simple pleasure of knowing my parents couldn't find me.

Byrd Baylor, author of numerous successful books, has used this theme for *Your Own Best Secret Place.*

"I was walking beside the river one day," she says, "and came upon this hollow tree with a sign on it saying, 'Keep Out.' So I went in. There was a blanket in there and some odds and ends in a little box. From then on when I was out walking, I'd always stop at that tree and sit in it awhile and wonder about the person who had left his things there and put up the sign. I thought about all the secret places I had as a child—and still have, as an adult—and how much they mean, what an important part of a person's life they are."

What are the places you remember from childhood? Can you reach back now and grasp for their magic?

Golden Agers are at the time for dreaming. They are natural what-iffers. What if the rubber raft you are playing on gets swept out to sea? What if the shadow at the window is a vampire? What if you could know what was going to happen before it happened? (I used that one for *A Gift of Magic.*) What if the plane that was taking you to visit your grandparents in Florida crashed in the middle of the Everglades and you alone survived?

Brett, at nine, wrote a marvelous story called "The Day the Sun Went Out" in which he had our whole family squeezed into a bathtub of hot water. It eventually froze, holding us prisoner, while we slowly starved. On the far side of the bathroom was a cookie jar, but we couldn't reach it. We grew more and more hungry and ate first the soap, then the washcloths, then the bath mat, and finally, just as starvation set in, Brett saved us by breathing hard on the ice and melting it enough so we could get loose.

This is the final stage of unisex reading, a fact you should take advantage of if you can. If you are able to put both boy and girl protagonists into your book you will enjoy a double sale. Once they reach the teens, there is a sharp dividing line between boys' books and girls' books; and although a girl will sometimes step across the line, a boy—never.

Books for the middle-aged child sometimes have illustrations, but they are usually line drawings and of minor importance. This is not the author's concern. If the editor wants pictures, he will hire an illustrator. Books for this age fall into the 40,000-word bracket, give or take 5,000, which gives you enough space to fully develop plot and characters. If you are a history buff, you are in luck, for biographies and junior novels with historical settings are in demand. So are books in which there is role reversal, with girls doing "boy things" and boys sharing in "girl type" activities.

Your hero or heroine should be at the top of the age group for which you are writing. For the Golden Agers, for instance, a good age for the protagonist would be twelve or thirteen. A ten-year-old can relate forward to an age he *will* soon be, but he would be bored with a "baby story" about someone younger than himself.

This is an age for humor. One of my more successful juveniles was a book called *Hotel for Dogs*, which I wrote as a sort of therapy. When my mother died, I was in the middle of working on an adult murder mystery. I found myself unable to complete it. The subject of death was suddenly too upsetting. For months I could not write at all. Finally, to force myself back to the typewriter, I chose a project as far afield as I could get from anything I had done before.

I picked my category—a humorous animal book—and tried to give myself as large a readership as possible by having sister and brother protagonists, ages eleven and thirteen. In the story, Liz and Bruce turn the vacant house next door into a home for neighborhood strays. Their efforts to keep this venture secret while dogs howled, barked, and bred seemed to hit the funny bones of a lot of children who may have harbored dreams of similar undertakings.

The Teenage Novel. This is my special field, and I am going to indulge myself by devoting the whole next chapter to it. Books here will run a bit longer than those for younger readers; 55,000 to 60,000 words is about average. There will be no illustrations other than the one on the jacket.

Although the young adult book is officially classified as "teenage" and is usually about seventeen-, eighteen-, and nineteen-year-olds, it will probably be read by those fifteen and under. The older teenager is generally reading adult books, although these may have teenage protagonists with whom he can identify.

The teens are an age for category novels: romance and career stories for girls, adventure and sports stories for boys, and mysteries for all.

They are also voracious readers of fantasy and science fiction. Dorothy Broderick, managing editor of VOYA (Voice of Youth Advocates), a journal devoted to reading and library services for adolescents, feels that this is because many adolescents have reached a stage at which they are capable of abstract thinking.

"They approach the fantastic in a different way than they did when they were younger," she says. "They are very much aware of the difference between a fiction story and reality."

Many teenagers are also mature enough to be able to appreciate the subtleties of mainstream novels in which character development is more important than action.

Payment is made differently to a book author than to the writer of magazine stories. While a magazine will purchase a story at a flat rate, the usual procedure for books is for the author to get an advance "against royalties." After receiving this, he gets no more payment until the royalties earned pass the amount of the advance. Once this occurs, he receives a statement and a check every six months.

Contracts vary, but it is customary for an author to receive 10 percent of the selling price of his book until it has sold about 10,000 copies, at which time the royalty will jump to 12½ percent and eventually to 15 percent. Income from secondary sales such as movie and television, magazine serialization, and foreign and paperback editions are divided between author and publisher as determined by each individual contract. While children's books do not often get made into movies, it does happen occasionally, and they often get picked up by book clubs such as Weekly Reader and Junior Literary Guild. In many cases they go into paperback so youngsters can order them through their schools.

You don't have to produce a book in order to write for children. There are more than 100 juvenile magazines and story papers looking for material. These vary in type almost as much as magazines for adults. There are juvenile literary magazines such as *Cricket*; specialty publications like *Nature Friend Magazine* and *Odyssey* (a magazine about astronomy and outer space); history magazines like *Cobblestone*; organizational publications such as *Boy's Life* (published by the Boy Scouts); and educational and entertainment publications like *Nautica—A Magazine of the Sea for Young People*, *Highlights for Children*, and *Humpty-Dumpty's Magazine*. There is a multitude of Sunday-school story papers published weekly by churches, and there are curriculum supplements such as *Current Health* and *Career World* which are distributed through the schools.

These magazines use all sorts of material—fiction stories, how-to's, educational articles, verse, and puzzles. One of my former students with a background in science has made a name for himself explaining today's modern miracles to the readers of *Highlights* in terms that children can understand. (The fact that he has two youngsters of his own is a help to him; he tries his material out on them before submitting it.) Another student, a nature enthusiast, shares her interest in regional wildlife with the children who read *Ranger Rick*. An African student wrote an adventure story laid in the fishing village of his childhood for *Primary Treasure*, a Seventh-day Adventist publication, and a Mexican-American student explained the custom of breaking pinatas to the readers of *Weekly Reader*.

You don't need to be a child psychologist to write for children. You need only to have been a child yourself, and to remember what it was like. The field of juvenile writing is a lovely one. Enjoy!

. . . When writing the text for a small-child's picture book, the writer must think in terms of scenes . . .

A child who dreams of horses
Flies fast and far at night
And travels miles of moon-trail
Before the sky grows bright.
She climbs the peaks of mountains
And struggles through the haze
Until she finds the canyon
Where dreamland horses graze.

The horses hear her summons
And race to heed the call.
They speed across the valley,
They leap the canyon wall.
Their manes are twined with flowers,
Their breath is sweet as hay.
A child can hear their hoofbeats
From many miles away....

(*Horses of Dreamland*, Little, Brown)

16. Writing for Teenagers

When I wrote *Debutante Hill*, it was returned for revision because in it I had a young man of twenty drink a beer.

"You can't do this," my editor wrote. "You can't mention liquor in a book for teenagers."

I changed the beer to a Coke.

Several years later I wrote a teen adventure novel in which a girl and her brother, fourteen and twelve, were engaged in a wild chase through New England in an effort to keep secret documents out of the hands of the "bad guys." Too exhausted to flee further, they stopped at an inn, rented a room, and slept for a couple of hours.

This chapter came back with exclamation marks in the margin.

"You have two members of the opposite sex sharing a room, and they're not married!"

"But they're brother and sister," I protested. "It's the middle of the afternoon with sunlight streaming through the windows. They're fully clothed, they're lying on twin beds, and they only stay a matter of a few hours."

"That makes no difference." my editor said. "Librarians

would never touch a book that included such a suggestive scene. You will have to let them rent separate rooms."

Since my characters were down to almost no money, I could not imagine their doing such a thing. Still, I didn't want to offend the nation's librarians. We finally reached a compromise—an L-shaped alcove in which the boy could nap out of sight of his sister.

Years later, when Don and I, our children, and a friend of Brett's all piled into one motel room on a family vacation trip, my thoughts went back to that editor. I gazed out across the bodies stretched wall to wall in various attitudes of slumber and was glad she was not with us to witness the sight.

I wonder too what she thinks about the subject matter of the youth novels of today. The young people's section of today's library contains books on alcoholism, drug use, social and racial problems, premarital sex, parental divorce, mental illness, and homosexuality. Judy Blume, whose youth books have reached a peak of popularity, lets her child characters pick their noses, torment each other, pad their training bras, and rehearse with their sanitary belts for the Big Day.

"I write the kind of books I wish I'd had as a youngster," Judy says.

The response of her young readers seems to prove that she has touched upon a universal need. "I thought I was the only one in the world who thought and felt like this," they write in a thousand letters a week. By drawing upon the memory of her own teen years, Judy has managed to bridge the gap between generations as though it did not exist.

And so can we all—for those years defy forgetting. Never before or after are we more vulnerable. I have a diary my mother kept in 1923, the year she was 17:

> I am so heartbreakingly lonely! I want to go to dances, to be rushed, to have letters and flowers and dates and proms! I am just one lie after another. When other girls talk about their beaux and their good times, I either keep still or make up a story of my own—something that might have happened to me, that should have happened to me—but never did.
>
> I'm so tired of bluffing! I want so awfully to have a good

time. While the football season is on I root for Princeton. And yet, whom do I know at Princeton? Russel Melcher. He was polite to me for two days because he is naturally polite, but did he hunt me up during the rest of the time we were in New York? No. Has he thought of me since then? Of course not. The girls are lovely to me, but does it ever occur to them to introduce me to the boys they know? Certainly not. Girls don't do that.

I read the entries written in that beautiful, lilting hand—people studied penmanship in those days—and the years fall away. It is myself I am reading about. It is one of my daughters. The world may have changed, but the basic emotions of youth have not.

So we reach within ourselves and find the makings for our story. What then? I hate to destroy the mood of the chapter by telling you, but I'm afraid I'm going to have to. We construct a plot.

If you will read and analyze a shelf of juvenile books, I think you will find that almost all of them conform to the following construction pattern:

Someone the reader likes overcomes increasingly difficult obstacles to reach an important goal.
Think back to the earliest fairytales in which the woodcutter's son slays a succession of dragons to win the captive princess. Update that to plucky Dorothy Gale combatting wicked witches and flying monkeys as she travels the Yellow Brick Road to the Emerald City in order to be returned to Kansas. Can you see the skeleton of the construction pattern fleshed out with characterization, description, dialogue, and individual style?

Or—take a lonely, sensitive seventeen-year-old girl like my mother in the year 1923. Her goal is to be popular. And in the way are the obstacles—her shyness, the fact that she is new in town, possessive girl friends who won't introduce her to the local boys—and the ego-shattering experience of being dropped by a boy named Russel Melcher, just when she thought he was getting interested in her.

In our modern teenage novels the plot may be quite sophisticated. The goal may be to gain an education or achieve in a career or simply for the hero to sort through the confusion around him and find a set of standards by which he can live. The formula, however, remains the same, and I would guess that nine out of ten rejected manuscripts are turned down by publishers because of a weakness in one of the elements.

Let's see how this might apply:

Someone the reader likes: The key word here is "likes." Our hero is the person in the story to whom our young reader must relate, and if he doesn't like him, he won't care much one way or the other what happens to him. If he does like him, he will follow him through 200 pages or so to see him safely wind up his adventure and reach his goal.

What is it that makes a reader relate positively to a character in a story? It helps if there is some similarity between the character and the reader. In general, a boy will want to read about boys, and a girl (with the exception of a few tomboys) about other girls. Age is important also. As mentioned earlier, the protagonist should be on an age level with the reader or on a level the reader can look forward to reaching soon.

A likable hero is attractive to the reader. What sort of people are you attracted to? My guess is that they are not total beauties. It's easier to resent a physically perfect person than it is to like him. Most of us are more comfortable with friends who do not overshadow us, but the defects in their looks should not be repellent. We can be attracted by a description of someone with a "round freckled face, a snub nose, and a mouth too wide for beauty," but "beady eyes set close together, a tight, pursed little mouth, and a nose with long black hairs scraggling out of it" is a bit more than the average person can handle.

The same thing applies to character traits. Which do you yourself find appealing? Which did you find appealing when you were a teenager? Leaf through your high school album, and react to the faces there. For which do you feel a sudden rush of warmth? Probably not "Miss Perfect" and "Mr.

Marvelous." To be human and lovable, a character must have some flaws, but here again, they should be attractive flaws. A shy person is engaging; most of us can relate to him. An impulsive, leap-before-you-look type calls forth smiles of sympathy. We draw back quickly, however, from the character who pulls wings off flies and poisons the neighbor's dog. If we attempt to make our hero cruel or two-faced or dishonest, we immediately lose all reader identification. Our reader does not want him to reach his goal, and he doesn't deserve to.

So our likable hero is an appealing combination of good and bad with the good far outweighing, and our reader is interested in him. He is pulling for him and wants him to succeed.

The important goal: What that goal is will be determined primarily by the type of book you are writing. In a mystery story the goal is automatic—to sole the mystery. In a career story it is to achieve success in a particular field. In a romance the goal is to win love. In an adventure story the goal is usually survival, and in novels of character development it can be an adjustment to life, a choice of values, or the establishment of a solid relationship with another human being.

If I were to write a book about my mother, using her diary entry as a jumping-off point, I might well decide not to make popularity her goal at all. A more realistic goal might be her realization that the Russel Melchers of this world aren't worth worrying over and that someday, when the time is right, love will come.

Did you keep diaries during your teen years? If so, go back and read them. Relive the intensity of your desires. Never again do we expect so much of life; never again are our joys and disappointments so extreme.

The goal you set for your hero or heroine must fulfill two requirements:

(1) It must be consistent with the age and interests of the reader (a ten-year-old boy couldn't care less about finding romance).

(2) It must be of real importance.

You know those little notes from editors that turn up on the bottom of rejection slips and say, "The plot is too slight"? What they are actually trying to tell us is that the goal is not important enough to the hero. John's desire to make the football team is hardly enough to keep a reader on edge throughout an entire book (though it might possibly do for a short story). If John does not make the team he will be disappointed, but his whole life will not be altered. Whether John wins a college scholarship or learns to walk again after his bout with polio or gets his wagon train safely through to California is another matter. These things do count. John's future hangs in the balance. These are strong goals and make for strong books of the kind that get published and keep selling year after year.

Look back upon those goals you set for yourself as a teenager. Which were truly important—and which did you only think were important? What are the goals that you, as an adult, wish to set for your own children?

If you are in doubt about the significance of your goal, ask yourself, "What would be the outcome for my hero if he didn't attain it?" Would the result be mere inconvenience? Or total disaster?

The increasingly difficult obstacles. The obstacles that separate our hero from his goal are what make things move. They are what make a "situation" turn into a "story." They can consist of almost anything—natural hazards (fire, flood, blizzard); bad guys (the kidnapper who holds his victims for ransom); good guys who don't understand (the well-intentioned parents who want Bob to go to law school when his dream is to become an artist). They can be poverty, race or sex (a black girl from a ghetto background who dreams of becoming a doctor), or a physical handicap (as with a homely girl who wants to win love).

The important thing about your obstacles is that they keep coming along in fairly rapid succession. If they do not, the rejection note will say that your story is "poorly paced." And it must be our hero himself who is the one to overcome the obstacles. He cannot lose his scholarship only to have rich Uncle Harry hand him enough money to cover tuition.

This then is a "formula." For those who shudder at the term, we may call it a "plan" or a "blueprint," but the meaning remains the same: It is the framework upon which the story is built. A hero or heroine—a goal—obstacles; they are three simple elements, but if one is weak the story is weak, and in today's market a weak story has little chance.

Within this plot framework, we can do anything we wish. We can invent fascinating characters, intertwine relationships, build mood and atmosphere, twist our readers' hearts or set them laughing. A formula does not necessarily restrict us. It does not tell us what to write about or how to write it. A book born from a construction formula can be as special as each mother's child is special and different from all other children in the world.

Although we have lost many of the early taboos in juvenile fiction, I don't want to imply that there are none at all. While sex and violence are no longer forbidden topics, they should not be sensationalized. And new taboos arise as old ones die. *Down a Dark Hall,* a teen gothic laid in a girls' boarding school, was returned to me for revision because the victims in the story were all female and the ghosts who terrorized them were male. Just as an earlier editor told me, "Librarians will never touch a book in which sister and brother share a room," my current editor said, "Women's Lib will never let you get away with making the girls all frightened victims." When I agreed to change the ghost of poe Alan Seeger to Emily Bronte, the book was accepted.

Another problem writers have to face when they write for teenagers is the fact that the novelist today is competing with television. When I was growing up, the one-eyed monster did not yet exist. Books were the only storytelling medium available, and I was more than willing to work my way through chapter after tedious chapter of description and character development in order to arrive at last at the action point of the story.

Youngsters today have been conditioned to expect instant entertainment. If something doesn't happen—and, I mean really *happen*—in the first three minutes of a television program, they flick to another channel. Because of this, today's authors of young adult books must utilize television techniques to capture and hold the attention of their audience. When I was writing *Killing Mr. Griffin* (a book about teenagers who kidnap their English teacher to give him a scare, only to have him drop dead of a heart attack while they're holding him prisoner), I knew the kidnapping would not take place until Chapter Six. Afraid my readers would not be patient enough to wait that long for excitement to occur, I used a "startle statement" hook to catch and hold them. My first sentence was: "It was a wild, windy southwestern spring when the idea of killing Mr. Griffin occurred to them." I hoped that, once they knew what lay ahead, teen readers would be willing to stick it out while I paved the way for the action scenes that were to come.

There are special joys in writing for teenagers. One is that it allows us to relive our youth and express at this later point in our lives the truths that we see in retrospect but could not then put into words. There is also the satisfaction that comes with planting seeds in fertile soil. Whether we are imparting information, planting values, or simply trying to instill a love of reading, we have a power when writing for the young that we do not have when writing for older, more blasé readers.

I realized this when I received my first fan letter. My first book had just been published. It seemed impossible that anyone could have read it yet. But, someone had.

This is the letter—written almost thirty years ago:

Dear Lois Duncan—
I have just finished reading *Debutante Hill* and will probably sound stupid to you since I am just a nobody, but could you possibly add on to the end of it? Say for instance have Paul and Lynn get married and something about the way the debuts turned out and what happens to Dirk and make Ernie and Nancy get married too? It does sound impossible, but just for me, please? Just one typed paper, please? I am so interested in this book I just can't stand it to be over. I must see another part of it. You won't have to send it to a publisher, just to me, please. I will be so grateful.
A faithful reader,
Barbara Scott

Barbara, wherever you are—thank you.

... It is myself I am reading about. It is one of my daughters. The world may have changed but the basic emotions of youth have not ...

Poems that bridge three generations:

> I am afraid, and I do not know why.
> I have a nostalgia for things I've never known.
> I have an aching and a hunger and a pain.
> I'd say it was a growing pain except that I am grown.
> An hour ago I sat beside a roaring fire
> In Chinese red pajamas with an apple and a book.
> Contented as a kitten that has curled by the fire.
> Contented as a dreamer who may dream with his book.
> And then I yawned and stretched and put my book away
> And opened up the window to a little new moon
> And a smell of the sea and the first hyacinth
> And I had a sudden aching pain for things I'd never known.

> (by Lois Foley, written in 1920, at age fourteen)

Her daughter:

> The sea and the sky have such great love
> That they run together in the evening.
> There is no line, so tender is their touch.
>
> I stand alone upon an empty beach
> And watch the gentleness of their embrace.
> I see a moon and stars shining from the water.
> I see the boat of some fisherman
> Sailing home through the sky.
> The sea and sky have such great love
> That they no longer are two separate things.
>
> I watch them—and I sigh and turn away.
> Lost in my silly dreaming, who am I
>
> To become jealous of the sea and sky?

> (by Lois Duncan, written in 1948, at age fourteen)

Her granddaughter:

> You sit in my mind
> Like a penciled drawing.
> Yet—
> There is still some hope
> That someday
> You may be erased.

> (by Kerry Arquette, written in 1970, at age fourteen)

Kerry's daughter Erin is one year old. What will *she* be writing, I wonder, thirteen years from now?

Converting your life experiences into mysteries, gothics, romances, and fantasy

17. Writing Genre Fiction

The class I taught at the university was scheduled early. During my first year on the faculty, I would arrive a good hour ahead of time to give myself a chance to go over lecture notes. My footsteps would echo in the empty halls, and the classrooms would be locked and silent. I would be absolutely certain I was alone in the building.

Then suddenly from an office at the end of the hall, like a burst of machine-gun fire, there would come the clatter of a typewriter.

No matter how early I was, journalism department chairman Tony Hillerman would be there ahead of me.

One morning I worked up the nerve to stick my head through the doorway and ask him what he was writing.

He said it was a mystery novel.

"You're writing fiction!" I exclaimed. It was the last thing I would have expected of a former newspaper editor and political reporter for United Press International. "Why, with your background as a journalist, I'd think you'd have all sorts of *nonfiction* material you'd want to utilize!"

"I do," Tony told me, "but this is the way I want to use it. I want to be able to twist it around and make things happen. There's a point when the inflexibility of facts becomes too confining. It's only in fiction that you have absolute control over your material."

"I can understand that," I said. "But, why write a mystery?"

"Because I want to *sell* it," Tony said simply. "I figured the best way to break into fiction would be with a genre novel."

This proved to be a lucrative decision. His book, *The Blessing Way*, was accepted by Harper and Row, the first publisher to whom he submitted it, and Tony went on to become a nationally recognized author of distinguished murder mysteries.

It's true that genre fiction (known also as category fiction) is easier to sell than mainstream. The main reason for this is that the readership is predictable. There are large segments of the reading population who hunger for one type of reading matter only and become so desperate when they are deprived of their literary "fix" that they will read almost anything the genre has to offer. Publishers know in advance what the demand is for various categories of genre novels and are always on the lookout for capable writers who can be counted on to produce on a regular basis.

Genre writing is always to some degree formula writing. Each genre has its own rules and regulations. Working within this framework, however, a talented writer should be able to utilize his personal experiences to produce stories which are his own and nobody else's.

Let's look at some of the more popular types of genre writing:

The mystery novel. Mysteries fall into two general categories, the "who-done-it" and the suspense novel. In the who-done-it, the viewpoint character is usually the detective. He is a more or less objective bystander who comes upon the scene after the initial crime has been committed and sets out to work his way through a maze of red herrings in order to solve it. In the who-done-it, the puzzle is all-important, and the characters are secondary to the plot.

In the suspense novel, the viewpoint character is someone involved in the story, and the threat of what may be going to happen is more important than what has already taken place. The most violent scene in a suspense novel usually takes place at its end, and our hero or heroine's goal is not so much to solve the mystery as to save himself. Because of this, characterization is extremely important; the reader has to understand and care about the hero in order to worry about his fate.

The mystery is perhaps the most tightly plotted form of fiction. It conforms to the letter to the plot formula: Someone the reader likes (our viewpoint character) overcomes increasingly difficult obstacles (red herrings, distractions) to reach his goal (survival and the disclosure of the villain's identity).

Because the strength of the story increases with the importance of the goal, the crime in the mystery novel is almost always murder. Anything less would make the goal comparatively meaningless. It does not matter, really, if a shoplifter is not caught and punished or if embezzled money is not located and returned. The world does not end. But if a murderer is allowed to run free, he is a threat to society—and more important—to the characters in the book with whom we have become emotionally involved. The world *will* end for his victims. When murder is the crime, the goal automatically becomes "survival."

My own mysteries have all been suspense stories, and all except one have been for teenagers. They have sprung from my life's straw and been spun by the "what-if" technique.

Most of the plot ideas have been triggered by minor incidents, unimportant in themselves.

An example: A conversation between Kerry and a girl friend that took place in the kitchen while I was fixing dinner. Kerry was chattering away about a "cool guy" she had met at a party, and the friend was trying to decide what to wear on a movie date. As the two-level conversation went on, each girl dropped the name of her man-of-the-moment, and to their dismay they discovered they were talking about the same boy.

The dual-identity situation intrigued me. It opened all sorts of doors in my mind. *What if* the boy had deliberately implanted himself in the lives of two girls he knew were friends? *What if* he built up a different personality to present to each of them? Why would he do such a thing? What might he hope to accomplish by such deception?

The idea eventually led to *I Know What You Did Last Summer*, a book about a man who wanted revenge for the hit-and-run death of his younger brother and who made himself a part of the life of each of the teenagers who had been in the death car.

Although the identity of the villain is concealed in the who-done-it, in the suspense story it is sometimes revealed quite early. Occasionally the suspense story is written from the viewpoint of the murderer, and the reader watches as he selects his victim, decides how to dispose of that victim, and carries out his scheme.

The suspense story gives the writer more freedom for experimentation than the traditional who-done-it with its pattern of events:

1. Murder, usually within the first several chapters.

2. Introduction of the hero, who is often the detective.

3. Gradual presentation of suspects and clues.

4. The hero's deepening involvement in the situation (he generally becomes romantically bound to either a suspect or the potential victim).

5. Heightening suspense, sometimes brought about by a second murder.

6. The climax, at which time the murderer's identity is revealed and the hero and reader both know at last "who done it."

Yes, it's a confining formula, but it is a successful one. The demand for mystery novels is unceasing. They are addictive. The typical mystery-enthusiast gobbles them up like popcorn, often latching on to an individual writer and devouring each of his books right down the line as fast as they can be consumed.

The gothic. The gothic, while it does always contain a mystery, is a genre all to itself. A fiction editor at *Good Housekeeping* describes it this way:

"A gothic is a romantic, suspenseful melodrama with standard ingredients: a damsel in distress (who is often a governess); a dark, brooding Mr. Rochester or Heathcliff sort of character; and an atmospheric setting such as an old mansion. The elements can be applied to a short story—Daphne Du Maurier has done some at that length—but it's rather difficult to handle in short form without turning it into a horror story. There should be room in a gothic for slow-paced development. A novelette is a good length for this sort of story."

The *Good Housekeeping* novelettes run 10,000 to 15,000 words.

The fact that the author must operate within this set of guidelines does not mean that he can't be creative within the restrictions of the formula. My own young adult gothic, *Locked in Time*, was inspired by Kate. Like clockwork, on her thirteenth birthday, my affectionate, cheerful, delightful youngest daughter became a hostile alien. No longer was I the beloved "world's best mommy." Everything I said and did was subject to criticism. No longer did we have intimate heart-to-heart mother-daughter chats; Kate was either snarling or sulking or plugged in to her Walkman.

"It's just a stage," I told myself reassuringly. "She'll outgrow it the way the other kids did. A couple of years from now we'll be good friends again."

That was the housewife-mother side of me talking. The writer side whispered, "But—*what if she doesn't outgrow it? What if she stays thirteen forever?*"

What would it be like, I asked myself, to be locked in time with a bitter, resentful teenager who never outgrew her training bra—who never got rid of her adolescent acne—and who held *me* responsible for having placed her in such a dilemma?

Drawing upon my childhood memories of Florida swamplands, I laid *Locked in Time* in the "atmospheric" Louisiana bayou country, where Nore, my seventeen-year-old "damsel in distress," is imported to spend the summer with her recently remarried father. As soon as she catches sight of the "old mansion" owned by her stepmother and her two teenage children, Nore senses that terrible danger awaits her there. The "dark, brooding" love interest is Nore's stepbrother, Gabe.

Having established all these essential elements, I was then able to have a good time with the freedom left to me. Nore comes to realize that her new family is not as normal as it seems. The mother had managed, through Cajun witchcraft, to halt the process of aging, and she and her children have been their current ages for a century. The psychological ramifications of rebellious teenagers, aching to leave the nest, yet dependent upon a parent for all eternity, made this book more fun to write than almost anything I've done. It also helped me put Kate's and my situation into better perspective. (Writers seldom need shrinks—their typewriters serve as couches.)

The romance. Like other genre novels, romances follow our standard plot formula—someone the reader likes overcomes increasingly difficult obstacles to reach an important goal. In the case of the romance, "someone the reader likes" is always an attractive, vulnerable young woman, and the "important goal" is to find love. The "obstacles" are problems and misunderstandings that keep the lovers apart until the final pages when they are neatly resolved to provide a happy-ever-after ending.

Romance novels fall into a long array of subcategories, ranging from the "inspirational" (a gentle kiss and a lot of prayer") to the "sensual" (erotic sex described in lurid detail). Publishing houses are happy to supply writers with tip sheets listing their own individual requirements.

Those of my friends who write romances seem to thoroughly enjoy it, and there are some of them who make a lot of money. In my own case, those personal experiences that take place in the bedroom seem a little *too* personal for me to feel comfortable sharing.

Fantasy. When I met Stephen Donaldson, he was in his twenties, living on little money and raising a teenage sister. He was also struggling to find a publisher for a novel he had written called *Lord Foul's Bane.*

I asked what the book was about.

"The hero is a leper," Steve told me. "He's socially ostracized, his wife walks out on him, and he keeps getting transported to a magical place called 'The Land.' He paused and then added, "I've written two sequels. I'm submitting the three books together."

The project sounded so hopeless I hardly knew what to say.

"Has any publisher shown an interest?" I asked, trying not to sound patronizing.

"Not yet," Steve said. "So far the books have been rejected forty-seven times."

Then lightning struck to create one of those success stories that make the writing profession such an exciting one. Steve, who had run out of new places to send his books, resubmitted them to Ballantine, the first publisher who had rejected them. Since the earlier submission, there had been a change of editors, and this time the trilogy was accepted. *Lord Foul's Bane* was named "Best Novel of the Year" by the British Fantasy Society and more than 700,000 copies were sold. Steve then followed his first trilogy with three more books about the same unfortunate leper. One of these, *White Gold Wielder,* hit the top of *The New York Times* best seller list, and Steve was poor no more.

Do personal experiences have a place in fantasy?

"Of course," says Steve. "Where else do you start any meaningful story except out of the depths of your own being? My father was a medical missionary, and I was raised in India where mystery and danger were a part of everyday existence. When I was sixteen, the worst age possible for such a transition, we moved to Ohio where I was expected to adjust to all the social mores of teenage America. The culture shock was as great as though I'd dropped in from outer space. That's the reason it was easy for me to understand and write about the problems of a misfit like Thomas Covenant, whose 'Land' was even more intimidating than an Ohio high school."

A second genre, closely related to fantasy, is science fiction. Although the writers of both are in the business of creating alternative worlds that are not like our own, the two terms are not interchangeable. In science fiction the worlds can be explained by science and technology, while in fantasy they can only be explained by magic.

Before meeting Steve, I was not aware of how popular the twin genres were or of how many writers there are who earn six-figure incomes by designing imaginary universes. Since then, however, I've come to realize how staggering their numbers are.

Steve feels that one reason for the recent leap in the popularity of fantasy is that people today feel a need to reassure themselves that human beings are strong and resourceful enough to cope with adversity.

"In fantasy, we don't play around with minor problems," he says. "We go straight for the monsters at the back of the brain. Readers find comfort in the thought that if a poor wretch like Thomas Covenant can take control of an alien world filled with evil magic, then surely, here in our more traditional world, there must be some hope for the rest of us."

If you are having trouble breaking into print with a mainstream novel, you might want to try your hand at writing in a genre. A lot of people make an excellent living writing category fiction and some genre novels are very fine indeed.

. . . A gothic is a romantic, suspenseful melodrama with standard ingredients; a damsel in distress . . . an atmospheric setting such as an old mansion . . .

We pulled through the gate into the drive beyond it. There, I found myself confronted by one of the most spectacular sights I had ever seen. On either side of the driveway, there stood a line of huge oak trees, their giant branches intertwining to form a massive canopy of vibrant green. Through the spaces between the leaves, the late afternoon sunlight fell in golden splashes, painting intricate patterns on the driveway below.

At the end of this incredible corridor, there stood what appeared to be a mansion, but, framed as it was by the immense trees, it was impossible to determine its true size.

The closer we drew, the more impressive the structure became. It stood three stories high, if you chose to count the groundfloor level as a story. The wide-porched main floor stood well above us and was supported by brick pillars and edged on both sides by a parade of graceful white columns.

"This is it," my father told me. "This is Shadow Grove."

"It's like something out of *Gone with the Wind!*" I exclaimed in amazement.

(*Locked In Time*, Little, Brown/Dell)

18. Keeping the Wheel Spinning

There are times in my life when I find I cannot write.

It is 8:30 a.m. Don has left for his office and the teenagers for school. Time to get to work. I go to my desk and wind a fresh sheet of paper into the typewriter. I sit there staring at it, a little shocked by its virgin whiteness.

Nothing happens. Nothing comes.

"Oh, no," I think, and know that I have come down with it again—the professional writer's disease—writer's block.

In my early days my reaction would have been pure panic.

"What's wrong with me? Something has happened! Whatever it was that made me able to write is gone!"

But I've finally come to realize this isn't true. A blocked writer *does* eventually write again. If you have it in you to write in the first place, you do not lose the ability, but you do become drained.

A writer's job is different from most others in that it cannot be done in any halfway manner. Everything you put on paper, whether good or bad, comes out of yourself. Every character you create is part of your own character, and every action that takes place occurs for you as well as for him. Bill Buchanan tells me that it took him days to write the final few paragraphs in the *Reader's Digest* version of *The Shining Season.*

"I wrote that death scene with tears rolling down my face; and afterward I was so emotionally spent I couldn't get up from the chair," he recalls.

Writing is a consuming and exhausting business, and after a period of constant giving, there must be a time for restoration.

I have noticed in myself that writer's block most frequently occurs after a time of emotional spending. When I first realized that I had found the man I was going to marry, I could not write; all my enthusiasm and joy was pouring outward, to Don and the world in general, not the written page. The same thing occurred after Robin was injured in a ski accident and after Brett was hospitalized for a lengthy illness. There seemed to be no feeling left in me for writing. I put words on paper, but they were lifeless. Everything I produced during those depression periods ended in the wastebasket.

The first thing to do when you find yourself a victim of writer's block is to accept it for exactly what it is; not the end of the world, but a rejuvenation period. *Let* yourself rest. Be good to yourself. Call it a vacation, if that makes you feel any better, but don't feel guilty. Go out and do the things you normally don't have time for, and, if possible, do them with other people. Writing is a demanding and lonely profession, so use this vacation time to catch up on the world outside. Go to lunch with friends, give a party, play tennis, take a little trip; attend lectures, go to the zoo, take a hike, go dancing. Every experience you have is grist for the mill. It is the "straw" that you will eventually turn into stories. This time of gathering experiences, of living, is, in its own way, just as important to your writing as the time you spend setting words on paper.

Sometimes the mere fact that you have stopped pushing will dislodge the block. Within a short time, ideas begin to bud again and nudge you toward the typewriter.

But there are also times when this is not the case. What is the answer when you have taken your break and are rested and energetic and ready to start work again, and you still find your mind blank? What can you do to give yourself the necessary shove to get started?

Here are some of the things that have at one time or another worked for me and for other writers I know:

An approach from a new direction. Begin something totally different from anything that you normally write. If your specialty is romance, try a science fiction story. If you write confessions, tackle a factual article. If you generally write for adults, try a juvenile; write a poem, an editorial, an easy-read book, some verses for greeting cards.

The project that started me writing again after the loss of my mother was a humorous book for children. I cold-bloodedly outlined it and *made* myself write it. The change of pace revitalized me, and by the time I was a third of the way into it the block was broken and the words were flowing easily.

On a happier note, after my first grandchild was born, I couldn't write either. The incredible fact that my daughter, Kerry, was now herself the mother of a daughter was so overwhelming that I could think about nothing else.

As a first-time aunt, Robin was as excited as I was. Since neither of us was in any state to concentrate, we decided to put our other activities on hold and create some lullabies for baby Erin. I wrote the lyrics, and Robin composed the music. Then Brett, who is a soundman with a band, recorded them for us with Robin doing the vocals. By the time we had the tape "Songs from Dreamland" completed, my brain was functioning again and I was able to get back to work on a book.

Playing editor. Take a fling at being editor instead of writer and go back through your files to see what old manuscripts might be made salable. Reworking a sagging story requires little inspiration and takes a different type of effort from that required for the original job of creation. If manuscripts have been sitting in mothballs long enough, you will find that you can approach them as though they were someone else's work. You can spot with the objective eye of an outsider exactly where the weak spots are.

In many cases this review work can produce sales. During one rewriting period I decided to experiment by changing four old stories, originally aimed at the women's slicks, from the third to first person. I submitted them to new markets, and three of them sold as confessions.

Even in the worst of stories there are usually parts worth salvaging. You find them rising like mountain tops from the bogged down areas around them. These high points can suggest story lines that lead you in new directions, and before you know it an idea has emerged that has you headed for the typewriter.

Borrowing enthusiasm. The block does not strike everybody at one time and, painful though it may be to contemplate, while you are sunk in inertia there are other people at the peak of their activity. Writer's block is not contagious, but enthusiasm is, and an evening of shoptalk with other writers can give you the shove that gets your gears turning. Perhaps there's a writers' group in your town or a creative writing class that can provide this stimulation.

In my hometown of Sarasota, local writers met for lunch once a week at a favorite restaurant. I was telling Tony Hillerman about this one day, and we decided to see whether such a thing might work here in Albuquerque. Tony talked to the manager of a centrally located restaurant and asked him if he would set aside a "writers' table" on the first Friday of each month. He then sent a form letter to the writers he knew in Albuquerque and nearby vicinities saying, "If you would like to break away from the typewriter and enjoy a little shoptalk, show up for lunch. No reservations necessary—just wander in around noon."

To our surprise, more than twenty writers turned up for lunch that first time. Each brought the names of other writers in the area. Word spread, and soon the "first Friday" lunches began to provide a meeting place not only for local writers but for those who might be passing through town or vacationing in the Southwest. We never know who is going to show up; there are always new faces, and there is always stimulating conversation.

Might such a thing work in your town?

Setting the mood. Some suggest a glass of wine and soft music to get in the mood for romance. I hesitate to go so far as to recommend wine before each writing stint, but mood music is not at all a bad idea, and mood reading may be even better. I am very much influenced by what I read, and a piece of good writing never fails to excite me with the thought, "Maybe someday I will write that well myself."

Once I have a project underway, I try to hold my recreational reading as closely as possible to the same type of literature I am working on—mysteries when I am writing a mystery, juveniles when I am working on a juvenile, etc.—and always the best in the field.

I learned my lesson about this one time when I submitted a first-person piece to *Good Housekeeping* and got a phone call from the features editor.

"What's happened to your style?" she asked. "You sound as though you've been writing for the confessions."

The fact was, I had been. I'd been switching an old romance from third person to first to submit to *True Secrets*.

I went to the library, took out the last six issues of *Good Housekeeping*, and immersed myself in them. Then I wrote the article. This time it sounded like a piece for the women's slicks.

Keeping a notebook. We seldom know at the time we experience them how particular events can best be put to use in our writing. Even if we do know, we may not have time right then to rush to the typewriter and produce an article or story. Creativity seems to come in spurts, and it is very likely that you will get swarms of ideas just at the time you are too busy to fully develop them.

If you can get into the habit of jotting ideas down to refer to later, you may find that by the time you get to them they have developed in your subconscious and are ready to spring full-blown onto paper.

Plotting does seem to work this way. It is a slow, measured, step-by-step process. You may not realize it yourself when your block begins to crumble. An idea comes to you, and though it is not an especially good one, you play around with it a little. You may begin to write it and discard the page. Another idea emerges, triggered by that first one. You mull it, release it, and turn to something else. The first idea comes back to you in a different form. It tugs at the edge of your consciousness. The underneath, hidden part of your mind gnaws at it while the upper part continues to move in other directions.

And then, suddenly one day, it all comes together. You get up in the morning, and it is there, shining and exciting, demanding to be set on paper. You go to your desk, and without an instant's hesitation, you begin to write. The words come quickly and surely, and you feel good about them.

And about yourself.

. . . we decided to put our other activities on hold and create some lullabies for baby Erin . . .

> The moon is wise,
> The moon is old,
> And all her songs
> Come wrapped in gold,
>
> The sweetest songs
> I ever knew—
> She has no child
> To sing them to.

(Oh, gentle moon—oh, lonely moon—
   I cannot bear your weeping—)

> The night is dark,
> The night is long,
> I know a child
> Who needs your song.

(Oh, gentle moon—oh, mother moon,
  My child will soon be sleeping—)

> The two of us,
> The moon and I,
> We sing our child
> A lullaby.

> (Songs *from Dreamland*, RDA Enterprises)

19. The PEs in the Bottom Drawer

Rejection slips!

I cringe as I type those words. No matter how well established a writer may become, he or she is never immune to the pain that accompanies rejection.

Some rejection letters are more dreadful than others. The absolute worst I ever read was sent to one of my university students when she was a sophomore in high school. It destroyed her self-confidence so completely that she didn't submit a manuscript to a magazine again until her senior year of college when she was forced to in my class.

Since the editor who wrote this letter was fired for doing so, I'll restrain myself from revealing the name of the magazine:

Dear Beth: The poem you submitted to us is pretentious, immature and lousy. Your accompanying letter is also ridiculous. What makes you think you have written anything that anyone would want to read, much less pay money for?

Is it any wonder poor Beth threw a cover over her typewriter and dropped out of the Roswell High School Creative Writing Club?

I have received more than my own share of rejection letters. In my office (which was once Kate's nursery and is still decorated in Early Sesame Street decor) between my desk and the wall, there stand two gray, metal filing cabinets. In the top drawers are letters from editors, contracts, book reviews, and tearsheets of published work. In the middle drawers are carbons of stories and articles now in the market—"hopefuls" that are bouncing busily around from editor to editor. Some will find acceptance; others will not. And eventually the ones that come back home to roost will find their way into one of the lower drawers. These are the failures, the stories and articles that didn't sell.

Why do I keep them? Because they are important.

Among these stories is a 1,200-word short-short called "The Fairy in the Woods," written when I was ten years old. This is how it begins (I've left the spelling intact):

> Sandy stood quietly watching her, watching her with large blue eyes because he was affraid she might dissapear like one of those lights you sometimes see on summer nights. Her hair was brown, a soft brown like the brown of a pine tree when the sap begins to run, and her eyes were dark and full of seacrets like the woods.
>
> "Excuse me," Sandy said softly, "but are you a fairy?"

This was not the first story I ever wrote, but it was the first that ever completely satisfied me. I don't remember how long it took me to write it, but I do remember reading it over with a feeling of wonder. Sandy, the fairy, the woods in springtime—they were all there exactly as I wanted them! I had made them myself, and I almost wept, they were so beautiful.

I sat down at my father's desk and, carefully, with one finger, typed out my story on Mother's best stationery. Then I mailed it to *Ladies' Home Journal*.

It is to the eternal credit of the *Journal* that they did not take one look at this offering and chuck it into the nearest wastebasket (I had not learned yet to enclose a self-addressed stamped envelope for a manuscript's return). Nor did they send it back with an impersonal, printed rejection slip. Instead, one of the editors wrote me a lovely letter in which he said that although the *Journal* could not use a story about fairies at the present time, the story itself was well written, and, please, for me not to stop writing but to work very hard at it, and the *Journal* would be there waiting for me when I grew up.

"The Fairy in the Woods" was certainly not fare for the women's slicks. That's beside the point. The important thing is that with this story I made my first tentative venture into the frightening world of literary competition and, luckier than Beth, I found it not so terrible at all. Editors were warm, friendly people who liked my stories (even when they did not publish them), and they were very concerned that I keep on writing; and that nice magazine and who-knows-how-many-more were just marking time, keeping themselves in business, until I was old enough to fill them with adult material.

With this kind of encouragement, how could anyone fail to keep on writing? As of that day my course was set. I never had the slightest doubt about what I was going to do or that eventually I could be successful.

There are many other stories in the bottom drawers of my file. Not all of them are as significant as the first, but all are important in some respect because of the things I learned through writing them.

There are six of them, for instance, that I wrote after my first "fluke" sale to *McCall's*. "Lisa and the Lions" had brought in $1,200—more money than I ever had believed existed. It was during the early days of my first marriage. My young husband was in law school, and we were living on the GI Bill. That *McCall's* check, zooming in out of the blue, was the answer to a prayer.

"Good Lord!" my husband said, stunned. "All that money for one little story! What are you waiting for, Lois? Write another!"

"But—" I said numbly, staring at the blank sheet of paper

in my typewriter, "—I—I can't think what to write about."

"Write a *McCall's* story," he insisted. "You know how; you've done it once. Now all you have to do is turn out another just like it."

It sounded reasonable enough, so I tried. And tried. And tried. I gave "Lisa" brown hair, red hair, and blond hair. I had her pretend to be a high-wire walker, a race-car driver, and an underwater treasure hunter. I had her interviewed for magazine features, newspaper articles, and television commercials. Every manuscript came back by return mail.

What did I learn? That you cannot write a story more than once and have it ring true. That one sale to a magazine does not mean that you are going to be able to slip right in the open door with a poor second. That there is no such thing, really, as a "*McCall's* story" or a "*Redbook* story" or whatever. Each publication has its definite wants, it's true, but these needs must be filled with fresh material, not tired, uninspired reruns, drained off the edges of past successes.

Not all the material in those bottom drawers is necessarily hopeless. Bits and pieces of it keep rising again. Very few stories are wholly bad. Some of them have good plots but need reworking, reorganizing, and polishing. Others have interesting characters, but need better plots to put them into action. It is hard to recognize these things when you have just finished writing a story, but if you pack it away for a few months and bring it out again, you have a better perspective. A number of my own "lost" stories have been revived at a later date. Others have provided me with dialogue, characters, and description for subsequent projects.

There was one scene, for instance, in which an unattractive teenage girl wakes to the murmur of voices under her window and looks out to see her younger sister saying goodnight to her date. Although she cannot make out their words, she can see her sister's hair shining gold in the moonlight and the darker shape of the boy by her side. Then the boy leans forward, and the light head disappears behind the dark one, and the older sister turns away from the window, filled with envy.

There is nothing so special about this scene; it's just that for some reason I always liked it. I tried to use it in two different short stories, neither of which made the grade. Finally, three years after it was first written, it became part of a book. It was not a minor part either, but set the scene for the entire relationship between the two sisters who were the book's main characters.

There is a story called "The Question" in one of those drawers. I wrote it when I was twelve. It's about a little girl named Dawn who insisted on believing in fairies long after she was too old to do so. The story drifts and wanders and is not very good, but there is a nice passage in it about the coming of night. One day, some twenty years later, I came across that story and was caught by that description. I rewrote the story from the viewpoint of the sensible, down-to-earth man who was Dawn's father. It went to *Redbook*.

My childhood piece of description was part of the new story.

There are book manuscripts in those drawers. Ten unsold preschool books are sitting there. So is a volume of poetry. There are two adult mystery novels that nobody wants to publish. One is hopeless, but the other has possibilities. Someday I may work that one over and see if it can be salvaged. There are the outline and first three chapters of a science fiction novel. I got that far and realized I was not cut out to write science fiction.

There are the first five chapters of a youth novel about a girl who gets involved in a religious cult. My editor at Little, Brown was enthusiastic about that idea. I was too, initially, and then, as I wrote, I came to see that I was not prepared to take on such a project. I have never been involved in a religious cult, and neither have any of my children. I couldn't make the cult leader generate the necessary charisma. The dialogue between him and his followers was flat and unnatural. Having no personal experiences on which to draw, I had no straw to spin, and I had to let the project drop. The theme of the book—a persuasive adult asserting pressure upon the minds of vulnerable youngsters—stayed with me, however.

Eventually I tried it again. This time I laid the story in the little Michigan town in which my husband Don was raised, and made the youth group a high school sorority and the adult an embittered man-hating woman teacher. Now I was on firm ground. I knew that teacher—and I knew the influence someone like her could have upon a group of young women (my daughters? my nieces?) struggling to find their places in a world of suddenly shifting values. The book came easily. I called it *Daughters of Eve*.

I am not alone with my drawers of "failures." All writers have them, and they have value. From these tries and failures and more tries, we learn to write the stories and books and articles that *do* sell.

Few writers who have the top drawer of their files filled with tearsheets of published work have lower drawers that are empty.

. . .I rewrote the story from the viewpoint of the sensible, down-to-earth man who was Dawn's father. My childhood piece of description was part of the new story . . .

"The Question"
(written at age 12)

Dawn was very wise. She knew about the elves and the fairies and the gnomes and all the tiny invisible little creatures that no one could see. She knew how the sun got up in the morning attached to a long golden string with five strong elves to hoist it up high into the sky and when they got tired to lower it gently into the ocean where it disappeared every night. She knew about the cloud fairies that drove the clouds across the sky, and the star fairies who lit the stars at night and blew them out in the morning, and the moon fairies who spread the moonbeams in long golden strips across the grass.

Of a truth, Dawn was very wise in the little folk and their ways. . . .

"True Believer'
(published in *Redbook* twenty years later)

". . .Look at the sun," Ellen says. "Isn't it beautiful?"

It *is* beautiful, bright and low, turning the sky orange behind the maples.

"Someday," she says, "I will have a dress that color, made of silk."

I turn to my wife, and she is smiling up at me with Dawn's green eyes—those wide eyes, misty with dreams—the eyes that see only what they wish to see. How did we produce a child like Dawn? How could I have asked such a silly question?

"I love you," I say softly. Usually she is the one who says it first, but tonight I am the one who says it.

I take her hand and hold it, and together we watch the sun go to bed, a sleepy red ball dropping behind the maples. Then the five strong elves light all the stars, and it is night.

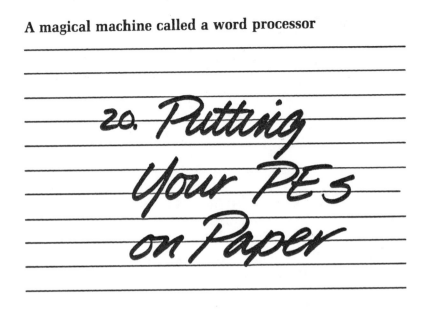

20. Putting Your PEs on Paper

A manuscript that is being submitted for possible publication must be typed. You can't get around this. If you cannot do the typing yourself, you will have to hire someone to do it for you. Even the neatest hand-printed copy will be returned unread by busy editors who have no time to waste on unprofessional offerings.

Use a black typewriter-ribbon and type on one side only of good quality bond paper. I suggest that you not use erasable bond because it smudges. All it takes is one editor with a damp thumb, and your beautiful story has had it. There is a correction tape on the market that will wipe out typing errors neatly. There is also a correction fluid. Both work well and are preferable to erasable bond.

There was a time, not very long ago, when this was the only possible way of completing a manuscript. The world has changed since then, however, and many professional writers have changed with it. We now have the option of writing with a computer.

When I was writing *The Third Eye*, a novel about a teenage psychic who helps the police locate missing children, I originally envisioned the story as being laid in the autumn with high school football games churning in the background and all the trees leafed out in gold.

A quarter of the way into the story, I realized that to advance the plot I needed to have a little girl drown in the Rio Grande. Since this is a river that runs fast and deep only in springtime, I would have to switch my autumn-based story to spring.

A year before, that simple change in season would have meant retyping sixty pages of manuscript. At that time, however, I had been using a regular typewriter. Now, I owned a magic machine that could take the drudgery out of a rewrite. In ten minutes time, I was able to go through the manuscript, locate the pages of description, and change gold leaves to green, football to softball, and even scatter around a few daffodils. Then I pressed a button on the keyboard, and the printer went into action, grinding out a nice, new, perfectly typed, springtime manuscript.

The Brave New World of the computer age has not only brought us video games, it has also altered the careers of thousands of professional writers who have forsaken their old-fashioned typewriters in favor of these miraculous machines.

A word processing computer looks deceptively uncomplicated and is composed of several standard parts:

A keyboard—much like a standard typewriter keyboard, although it does contain a few extra keys for issuing special commands;

A monitor—which is the television screen on which words are displayed;

An information storage medium—usually "floppy disks," flat, six-inch disks which resemble tiny phonograph records;

Disk drives—which are what allow you to store and retrieve information;

A printer—which actually sets your words on paper when you are finished with your composition;

Software—the program that tells the computer what to

do. This is usually on a floppy disk, which is inserted into the machine every time you turn it on.

My own word processor is to real, hardcore computer users what an Easy Read book would be to graduate students in English literature. I am a nontechnical person who can barely manage to get a plug into a wall socket, and I wanted the simplest, easiest-to-operate machine available.

Even so, my writing output has almost doubled because of the things my computer can help me with. Among these are the following:

1. Revising manuscripts. Although most authors have the basic plots of their novels laid out in advance, during the writing process characters will often take on lives of their own and develop in ways that were not part of the original plan. When this occurs, the author has to go back and make adjustments in early chapters to coordinate them with the later ones.

An example: In my young adult novel, *Stranger with My Face*, I created a character named Jeff who was to be the love interest for my teenage heroine. When I began the book, Jeff was a conventionally handsome boy; and then, when I was halfway into the novel, I got an idea for a way to make him more interesting. I decided to give him a scarred face. This meant going back through the early chapters of the book and changing every section in which Jeff's looks were referred to. It also meant altering his personality to reflect the emotional damage that the physical disfigurement had caused. With the help of the word processor, I was able to make these changes quickly and easily and could also insert a full-page flashback detailing the accident that had produced the scarring.

With a word processor, not only may material be inserted into a manuscript, it may be transferred from one of its pages to another. If, after writing a story, I read it over and realize that there is material on page 72 that would be better on page 3, I can lift that section of the story and move it. I can even open a space for it in the middle of a paragraph, insert it, and close up the gaps.

2. Cutting and expanding. A professional writer must tailor stories to fit the length requirements of the markets to which they are to be submitted.

An example: I recently researched an article on teenage alcoholism which is currently under consideration at *Ladies' Home Journal*, a magazine that uses lead articles of 4,000 words. If the *Journal* decides to reject my manuscript, the next place I will submit it will be to *Woman's Day*, a publication that seldom uses articles longer then 3,000 words. If I don't place my story there, I might want to try it on *Current Health*, which uses 2,500-word articles, or on *Woman's World*, which uses short features of 1,500 words or less.

In the old days, I would have had to retype the entire manuscript for each new submission. Today, I will be able to display the article on the screen of my word processor and cut and edit it, removing extra wordage by cutting adjectives and combining sentences and paragraphs, until I get it down to the right length. Then, all I will have to do is push the "print" button. I can repeat this process after every rejection, adjusting the length to fit each publication until the story has been accepted or until I've hit every national market that seems appropriate.

3. Changing names. Naming characters is always a challenge. Occasionally, a first and last name will leap into an author's head and sound totally right together. That occurred for me when I was writing *Killing Mr. Griffin* and needed a name for the teenage psychopath who caused the death of his English teacher. It wasn't until I had completed the book and was ready to submit it to a publisher that the horrible realization struck me that the reason the name had come so naturally was that it belonged to a boy on Donnie's Little League team.

I didn't want the boy's parents to sue me, so I spent two full days combing through the manuscript, crossing out the real name and replacing it with a fictitious one. Even so, I missed a few places and was embarrassed when a proofreader caught them later.

That was before I owned a word processor. If, at that time,

I'd had a computer that was programmed to make word substitutions, I could have asked the machine to do the whole job for me.

4. Correcting spelling errors. The machine can do this also! All you have to do is press a button and—zip!—every "embarassed" has the second "r" inserted in it!

5. Correcting typing errors. No White-Out or Correct-o-Type need be purchased if you are the owner of a word processor. You see the error on the screen and type right over it; the wrong letter is automatically replaced by the right one.

6. Storage. The filing cabinets in my office are filled to overflowing with copies of every article and story, published or unpublished, that was the product of the typewriter I used for three decades. With the increased output that I'm now getting by using the word processor, I would be crowded out of my office—perhaps, even, of our house—in a very short time if I continued to keep on storing carbons of everything I wrote.

That won't happen, however, for the material that goes into the processor is recorded on floppy disks even smaller than 45 RPM records. But on one of the more powerful systems, one disk will hold enough words to comprise an entire novel. I could continue to write, night and day, for the next hundred years, and still not require any more storage space for these manuscript disks than a bureau drawer.

I, myself, am not a person who moves easily with progress. It took years for me to talk myself into making the simple switch from a manual typewriter to an electric one. The switch to a word processor was an even more difficult move, and I still have not adjusted completely to my new acquisition. It may always seem a bit strange to me not to be setting words directly onto paper but onto a lighted screen that displays only a third of a page at a time. Even so, the conveniences my computer provides far outweigh any disadvantages produced by my own personal hang-ups, and it has more than paid for itself with the proceeds from my increased production.

There are writing machines today that make mine look like a baby's toy. One friend of mine who writes technical articles has his machine plugged into a data bank in Chicago, and whenever he has a question that requires research, he types it onto his screen, presses his "Call" button, and sees the answer appear instantaneously before his eyes.

Another friend writes romance novels. She has hundreds of romantic scenes stored on disks, and whenever she wants a love scene in a book she is writing, she calls one up on the monitor. Then she changes the hero and heroine's names and hair color, does a small bit of rewording, and inserts the scene into any spot in which she needs it. She turns out six books a year, and they take their turns topping the paperback best seller list.

Where are we going from here? It's hard to imagine. I would hate to think that there will one day arrive a time when novels will be written by robots. But I don't believe that will happen; robots don't have personal experiences to write about. The stories that live are the ones that are born of people who have things to say to other people, and no machine in the world, no matter how sophisticated, can duplicate that. What machines can do and are doing already, is help human beings write more easily and effectively by allowing them to concentrate on creative storytelling rather than on the functional process of setting words on paper.

> **. . . I was able to go through the manuscript, locate the pages of description . . . change gold leaves to green . . . and even scatter around a few daffodils . . .**

When she opened the door, the brilliant beauty of a New Mexico autumn burst full upon her, crisp and sparkling and radiant. The poplars that lined the yard glowed like golden candles against the rich blue of the sky, and a slight breeze rustled through them, making them shimmer like aspen. The lawn was beginning to lose the lush green of summer, but the dahlias and marigolds that bordered the slate rock path that led from the driveway to the house were a glorious profusion of red and burgundy and gold.

(from the autumn version of The Third Eye)

When she opened the door, the brilliant beauty of a New Mexico spring burst full upon her, crisp and sparkling and radiant. The rains that had fallen so heavily during the early part of the week had left the air fragrant and fresh. The poplars that lined the yard glistened pale green against the rich blue of the sky, and a slight breeze rustled through them, making them shimmer like aspen. The lawn still held the brown of winter, but the daffodils and crocuses were like bright flags, bordering the slate rock path that led from the driveway to the house.

(from the spring version of The Third Eye, Little, Brown/Dell)

21. Peddling Your PE's

So your article, fiction story, novel, or "small stuff" is written, revised, polished, and as perfect as you are capable of making it. What do you do now?

Well, you have two choices. You can tuck it away in a drawer and forget about it, or you can share it with others.

No—wait—there is a third alternative, but I doubt if many writers would choose to take it.

I was once a speaker at a writers' conference where all the participants submitted manuscripts along with their registration forms. These were judged, and the authors of the best were awarded free tuition.

That year the grand prize went to a huge and richly realistic novel about life in a mental institution. When the conference director phoned to give the winner the happy news, he was startled to discover that the story was autobiographical. The author was an inmate at just such an institution, and two attendants escorted him to the awards dinner.

The judge for novels was an editor from one of the top publishing houses in the country. He was so impressed by the manuscript that he phoned home and was given permission to offer a contract.

"This is really a red-letter day for you, sir," he told the author grandly. "We want to publish your book!"

"That's nice of you," the writer said, "but I just burned it."

When the stunned editor asked incredulously, "Why?" the author said simply, "I was through with it. Now it's time for me to start on something else."

Unlike that author, most of us want our work to be read. We want it to be published.

How do we achieve this?

Here are some of the questions I am asked most often by writers who are trying to cross the line to become professional:

In what form should a manuscript be submitted?

On the first page of your manuscript, type your name, address, and Social Security number in the upper left corner. In the top right corner, identify your submission (is it article or fiction? Sometimes with personal experience pieces or fiction stories that are written in first person it is hard for an editor to tell) and put the approximate number of words, correct to the nearest hundred. I have not yet been able to figure out any way to arrive at this figure in any absolute manner without counting the words. With a lengthy manuscript you can probably get a pretty good estimate by counting the words on four or five pages, getting an average, and multiplying.

The title of your story should be centered about a third of the way down the page. Under this, put "by" and then whatever name it is you wish to have your story appear under. If you are going to use a pseudonym, this is the place to put it.

Double-space your story and leave good margins, at least 1¼ inches on the left and 1 inch on the right. Try to keep your right margin fairly even. The whole idea is to make the manuscript as neat and attractive as possible. If you were sending your child out to look for his first job, you would see to it that his hair was combed and his face was washed. Do not do less for your manuscript. It, too, is seeking employment.

On your second and future pages, type either your last name or the title of the story at the top left corner and place the page number at the top right corner. Then drop down a few lines and continue typing your story. At the end of your final page you can put ### to show that the story is finished. The identifying byline or title at the top of each page is important. Editors go through a lot of manuscripts. If, at a day's end, someone finds a single page on the floor under a desk and it lacks identification, there is no way in the world for him to get it back into the right envelope.

Do not bind your manuscript or submit it in a folder. You may, if you wish, use a paper clip, but not a staple. Use a fairly loose clip and be sure that it isn't rusty. It will be removed and replaced in a different spot, and you would prefer that it not leave marks. After the fourth or fifth submission, paper-clip marks can become lined up like notches on a shotgun, so that each new editor can tell at a glance how many times the manuscript has been rejected. This shouldn't affect his reaction to it, but I can't help but believe it produces some sort of psychological effect.

Always retain a copy of your story. If you are using a typewriter, make a carbon; if you are using a word processor, save your story on to disk and keep a backup duplicate disk just in case. Manuscripts have a way of getting lost in the mail. Even if your story does make it through safely and is purchased, you may be asked to provide an extra copy for the illustrator to work from, so you want to be sure you have one available.

How do I mail my manuscript?

Any manuscript over three pages long should be mailed flat in a manila envelope. Enclose a second envelope, stamped and self-addressed, for its return if it is not accepted. You can enclose a short cover letter if you wish. This is important if your original query received a go-ahead, for you will want to remind the editor of this fact; otherwise the story might be rejected by an incompetent first reader and never make it to his desk.

Poems should usually be submitted several at a time, centered on the page and double spaced. Instead of the word count in the top left corner, give the number of lines.

Book manuscripts should be boxed and submitted with a

cover letter. Postage and self-addressed labels should be enclosed for their possible return.

The cheapest way to mail your manuscript is special fourth class rate, marked "manuscript." The person behind the counter at the post office will tell you that you cannot do this. Insist that he look it up in his book of postal regulations. The rule will be there, in your favor.

My own preference is to pay a little more to mail manuscripts first class and have them reach their destination more quickly and in better shape.

Should I use a pen name?

Do you have a reason for wanting to use one? In my own case, I had the same name as my mother, who was also a writer. When I sold my first story, I didn't want her taking credit for it (and she didn't particularly *want* credit for something written by a thirteen-year-old), so I decided to write under my middle name, "Duncan." By the time I married, I had sold enough stories under this name and established enough contacts so that I didn't want to start all over again. I retained "Duncan" as a business name and use my married name socially.

Here are some other reasons you might choose to use a pen name:

1. Your real name is such a difficult one that nobody will ever be able to pronounce, spell, or remember it.

2. Your name is totally wrong for the sort of things you are writing. (You're Rachel Greenburg and are writing articles for Catholic publications.) A woman writing for the men's magazines might want to use a masculine sounding name or simply use initials.

3. You are writing something highly personal and would prefer to protect your identity to avoid embarrassment for yourself and your family.

4. Your name is identical to that of somebody who is in the public eye. This can make for confusion. I thought for years that the writer Elizabeth Taylor and the actress by that name were the same person, and I was awed by the woman's diversity.

5. You are such a prolific writer that you are beginning to compete with yourself. An editor may want to run two of your stories in the same issue of his magazine, but may not want it to appear that the whole publication has been written by one person. In this case, you would probably want to have one story appear under a pen name. The same problem can occur if you have two books published in the same year. Librarians might decide not to purchase more than one book by the same author.

6. You are writing several types of conflicting material (children's books, perhaps, on the one hand, and hard-core pornography on the other), and you want to keep these two sides of your life separate.

If none of these reasons applies, I should think you would want to use your own name. Half the fun of being published is having your family and friends proud of you, and this cannot be accomplished if no one knows that the author of that masterpiece is you.

How important is it to meet editors in person?

I don't honestly know. I have been to New York three times in my life, twice on family vacation trips and once as a participant in an educators' seminar sponsored by the American Society of Magazine Editors. On that third trip, I met a lot of editors very quickly, and while it was a fascinating experience to get a behind-the-scenes look at the publishing business, I didn't suddenly start selling all these people my work just because I was now a face to them rather than a name on a manuscript.

The most important thing this trip did for me was to bring home with total certainty the tremendous differences between publications.

At *Ms.* we were greeted by a friendly receptionist in overalls and spent a morning sitting around a huge coffee-stained table, conversing informally with the managing editor and her staff, while children on tricycles zoomed up and down the hall outside the meeting-room door.

At *Redbook* we were offered a formal presentation complete with a short movie demonstrating *Redbook's* effect upon the eighteen- to thirty-two-year-old reader.

At *Time-Life* we sipped cocktails and feasted on shrimp, while at *Newsweek* we were given a tour through the wire and computer rooms.

At *Woman's Day* we visited the kitchens where the staff cooks were experimenting with recipes. In the background was the sound of sawing and hammering as carpenters constucted whole rooms which would be photographed for "before and after" decorating shots and then torn down so new rooms could be built for the next issue.

At *New York Magazine* we drank iced tea with a lively group of editors, none of whom looked older than twenty.

At *McGraw-Hill* we dined on filet mignon and drank wine in one of their many luxurious formal dining rooms.

At *Good Housekeeping* I walked down a hall over sections of carpet being tested for endurance to see which, if any, deserved the *Good Housekeeping* Seal of Approval and spent a relaxed hour in the charming, homelike office of the fiction editor. "We're looking now for a short-short about Thanksgiving," she told me. As soon as I got home, I wrote one.

The trip was an adventure I'm glad I had. It was nice meeting in person people who until then had been only names on a masthead. But it wasn't necessary for me to take that trip in order to write professionally.

Do I need an agent?

Probably. But that doesn't mean you're going to get one. Finding a good agent to represent you is at least as difficult as finding a good publisher. Most legitimate agents work on a commission basis. If your agent sells a story for you, he takes 10 percent; if he does not sell the story, he gets nothing. Naturally most agents are picky about whom they will represent and would like it if a writer was already selling with some regularity to the high-pay markets before taking him on.

There are some agents who are willing to work with beginning, nonselling writers, but these usually charge reading fees. Their income is primarily a result of these fees, not commissions, so they have little reason to strive hard to make sales for their clients.

The best bet, in the beginning, is to market your work yourself. It is far from impossible; in fact, it is done all the time. I have an agent who handles book contracts, but I still market my magazine stories myself and enjoy doing it.

You can learn a lot from author-editor contact. After a few letters back and forth you find yourself on a first-name basis and feel that you are working together as friends and partners for the benefit of both. You want to produce material that will sell, and your editor wants you to produce material he can buy. You both have the same goal, and a good editor who is willing to spare the time to offer occasional advice and encouragement can be invaluable to your development as a writer.

How do I go about copywriting my work?

Under the new copyright law, effective since January 1, 1978, an author's work is automatically copyrighted the moment he creates it. You, and you alone, have the legal right to print and distribute copies of your articles, stories, poems, and novels or to sell that right to others.

If someone does pirate your material, which is a relatively rare occurrence, and you want to bring an infringement suit against him, your work must be registered with the Copyright Office. It is possible to register it after an infringement occurs, but with after-the-fact registration, you can sue only for actual income lost because of the infringement. In order to sue for statutory damages and to recover attorney's fees, your work must have been registered before the infringement took place.

The process through which you can register copyright is to request the proper form from the Copyright Office and send this with a $10 registration fee and one copy of the work (two if it has been published) to the Register of Copyrights, Library of Congress, Washington, D.C. 20559.

What should I know about rights? Do different publications buy different kinds?

Yes, they do. A publication will indicate on acceptance what rights it will buy. Many magazines buy "All Rights." This means that from then on they own the material they have purchased, although they may, on request, permit you to have it reprinted elsewhere after publication. Others buy 'North American Serial Rights." This means that you retain foreign rights and can sell your story to publishers in other countries. "First Rights" means that the magazine is purchasing the right to publish your material for the first time, but that you can then offer "Second Serial (Reprint) Rights" to a digest publication.

If you are offering specific rights, such as "Second Serial Rights Only," because the story has already been published elsewhere, you should indicate this on your manuscript up at the top right corner along with the wordage, and also in an accompanying letter. If you do not do this, the magazine to which you submit your story will assume that all rights are available and will make their own decision as to which rights to buy.

Often the rights being purchased will be stamped on the back of the check you receive in payment. By endorsing the check, you will automatically be signing an agreement. Be aware of this, and don't get so carried away with the excitement of a sale that you cash the check without reading what is written on the back of it. It is important to know exactly which rights you are selling and which you retain.

One thing to look out for on a contract is the term "work-for-hire." Work-for-hire is work done on commission for someone else, and when you sign such a contract, you are signing away your copyright.

There are two kinds of work-for-hire. One is work that is done on the job by an employee of a company. If, for instance, you are a reporter for the *Podunk Tribune* and happen to witness the Second Coming during your workday, the story you write about it will become the property of the *Tribune*. They, not you, can sell second rights to *Reader's Digest*.

The other sort of "work-for-hire" is commissioned writing that is explicitly termed a "work-for-hire" *at the time of assignment*. Many writers are unaware of this and naively sign away all their rights to work that they submitted, not on assignment, but on speculation. There are publishers who routinely demand that writers of unassigned submissions sign work-for-hire agreements before they will pay them. In my own case, the devotional that appears in Chapter Twelve was already at the printer when I was presented with a contract that termed it a work-for-hire. I refused to sign it. If I had done so, I would not have had the right to use the piece in this book.

Can I submit the same story to two different publishers?

Not at the same time. You can imagine how messed up your life would become if both decided to buy "All Rights" to your story. Submit your material to the top-paying market on your list, sit back, and wait. If it is rejected, send it to the second market. It may take longer to make a sale this way, but it is a great deal safer.

The one exception to this rule is if you are submitting a story to a magazine that will purchase "Multiple Submission Rights." Some of the religious publications will do this, because they realize there is no overlap in readership (the readers of Catholic, Methodist, Jewish, and Baptist publications are not going to be the same people). If you do decide to submit your story to several such publications at the same time, indicate on the manuscript and in a cover letter that this is a multiple submission. A magazine that buys such a submission will pay less for it than if exclusive rights were offered.

With a book, you may be able to get a contract on the basis of an outline and several sample chapters. When the contract is signed, you will receive a portion of the advance (usually half). The remainder will be paid you on delivery of the completed manuscript.

When can I expect to be paid?

Most magazines pay on acceptance. There are some, however, that pay on publication. This means that they can accept your story and hold it indefinitely without paying you and without printing it. Steer clear of such publications if possible, but, if you do place a manuscript with one of them, ask for a written guarantee that if publication and payment do not occur within a set time (six months seems appropriate to me), you will be allowed to withdraw the manuscript and submit it elsewhere.

How long will a magazine hold my manuscript before accepting or rejecting it?

This depends upon the magazine, the number of people on the staff, and the amount of material that is piled on their desks at the moment. It is generally safe to assume that no news is good news and that the longer a story is held the more seriously it is being considered. This is not always true, however. I have had manuscripts held for over a year and then returned with nothing more than a printed rejection slip.

If two months go by without a response, I think it is appropriate to write a polite note asking if they have "reached a decision yet on my story" (and give the title), "which was submitted for your consideration on—" (and give the date). You don't want to antagonize an editor by being overly pushy; you might push him into a rejection when, given longer to consider, he would have talked himself into making a purchase. At the same time, there is always a chance that your manuscript was lost in the mail or has been misplaced by the editor and is sitting in an "out" basket on a vacant desk.

What sort of records should I keep?

Keep as complete a set of records as possible. Some writers keep a card file with a card for each story and make notations each time one is submitted, returned, or sold. Other writers keep the information in a notebook. The method you use is unimportant, but you do want to keep track of what has been submitted where—and when. When a story is sold, you will want a record of the rights that were purchased and how much you received.

Keep track of your expenses. You can deduct them on your income tax. As a writer, you own your own business and will be filling out the form for the self-employed. It doesn't matter if at first your writing income is small; plenty of beginning businesses operate in the red for the first few years. As long as you have a record of your submissions and can back them up with rejection slips, you can prove that you are "in business."

Business expenses may include paper, envelopes, typewriter ribbons, and repair; a portion of your house payment or rent, and heat and electricity, if you have a room which you use as an office; transportation to and from interviews, library, or post office; writers' magazines and conferences; research materials; long distance phone calls to editors; and, of course, postage. If you have to hire a typist or have photographs processed to illustrate articles, the cost of these can be deducted. Large items such as your desk, filing cabinet, and typewriter can be depreciated. I know one writer who deducts everything from the light bulbs in the lamp by her desk to the wear and tear on the vacuum cleaner every time she cleans the room she uses as an office.

My mother used to deduct the cost of keeping the dogs in a kennel whenever she and my photographer-father were away on assignments. She got caught one year by the IRS. I wouldn't advise going quite that far.

How many times should I submit a manuscript and get it back again before giving it up as hopeless?

As long as you still have faith in a story and there are still markets to which you can submit it, keep going. One adult novel I wrote on a controversial subject was rejected by one publisher after another for eight years. It was serialized in England, and versions were published in the Scandinavian countries, but no one in the United States would touch it. Finally, my agent placed it with Bantam as a paperback original, and I spent a week on revisions, updating hair styles, shoe styles, slang, etc.

Bantam then turned around and offered hardcover rights to the Doubleday Bargain Book Club. Doubleday, forgetting they had rejected the book years before, decided to accept it. The book then sold close to 300,000 copies.

Personal experience writing is not for everyone. A journalist-friend regards me with horror.

"How can you do this?" he asks. "How can you expose yourself this way?"

A friend who is a successful novelist has similar feelings.

"I keep my writing free of my personal life," she says. "No one who reads my books has any idea who I am—whether I am married—whether I have children—what I do when I am not creating."

The personal experience writer is always creating. When he isn't actively writing, he is gathering straw. This is his way of life. Each time I go to the mailbox, it is like Christmas morning. What will be waiting there? Has Santa really come? Will the account of something that happened to me three months ago have turned miraculously into a check?

The girl in the fairy tale who spun straw into gold had to agree to sacrifice her firstborn child. I have not had to do this. I am lucky in having a family that understands.

One night Don and I and our friend Isabel went to hear Robin, who was singing cocktail hours at the Hilton Hotel. Isabel has known our children since they were toddlers. Gazing across the room at Robin, poised and lovely, competently adjusting her microphone, she must have recalled as I did the gawky, snaggletoothed child who sang in perfect harmony as I strummed a secondhand guitar.

She covered my hand with hers.

"I know how you must feel," she said. "With all that talent, she should be back in college, getting a graduate degree in music, preparing to do something important with her gift."

I knew what was behind her reaction. Isabel was newly widowed with children to raise. She was grateful she had a master's degree and a teaching certificate to fall back on.

Before I could respond, Robin began to sing.

First, a song from her childhood; one we used to do together on summer nights in lawn chairs in the backyard.

Then a funny song Don likes, full of silly puns.

And then—

"The first time—ever I saw your face . . ."

It was their song, Isabel's and her husband's. At so many family gatherings Isabel herself had sung it, smiling across at the stocky, bearded man with the gentle eyes. At a Thanksgiving we celebrated together. At an anniversary party. At a mountain picnic.

The sweet, young voice reached out across the years and rested lightly upon us, and behind the words came the meaning—

We remember. We care. We loved him too.

A stranger at the table next to us blinked back tears. Beyond her, a man turned to the woman beside him and smiled. The experiences we were reliving were not theirs, but that did not matter. As each of us found his own memories, we were drawn close.

"Maybe I was wrong," Isabel said when the song was over. "Maybe she's doing what she's made to do."

Perhaps she is.

Perhaps, I, too, am doing what I am made to do. I know my sort of writing is unlikely ever to bring me the Pulitzer Prize, as my childhood mentor MacKinlay Kantor's writing did for him. But it does allow me to reach out to people I have never met and share those things that matter to me.

Those things are important, as Isabel's love song is important. They are what life is all about.

They are the gold.

# # #

Index

About the Author

Lois Duncan has drawn upon her personal experiences to sell more than 400 articles, stories, and poems to national publications including *Good Housekeeping, Ladies' Home Journal, McCall's, Redbook,* and *Seventeen.* She is the author of more than thirty books and has received "Young Readers Awards" from California, New Mexico, South Carolina, and Indiana; the Dorothy Canfield Fisher Award from Vermont; the Ethical Culture School Award from New York; the Zia Award; the Seventeenth Summer Literary Award; and three "Special Awards" from the Mystery Writers of America. One of her novels, *Summer of Fear,* was made into an NBC "Movie of the Week." She taught magazine writing for eleven years at the University of New Mexico and is a former Grand Prize Winner of the *Writer's Digest* Creative Writing Contest.

A homemaker and mother of five, she decided to supplement her practical experience with a formal higher education and graduated from college at age forty-two.

Other Books of Interest

General Writing Books

Beginning Writer's Answer Book, edited by Kirk Polking (paper) $12.95
Getting the Words Right: How to Revise, Edit and Rewrite, by Theodore A. Rees Cheney $14.95
How to Become a Bestselling Author, by Stan Corwin $14.95
How to Get Started in Writing, by Peggy Teeters (paper) $8.95
How to Increase Your Word Power, by the editors of Reader's Digest $19.95
How to Write a Book Proposal, by Michael Larsen $9.95
How to Write While You Sleep, by Elizabeth Ross $14.95
If I Can Write, You Can Write, by Charlie Shedd $12.95
International Writers' & Artists' Yearbook (paper) $14.95
Just Open a Vein, edited by William Brohaugh $15.95
Knowing Where to Look: The Ultimate Guide to Research, by Lois Horowitz $18.95
Law & the Writer, edited by Polking & Meranus (paper) $10.95
Make Every Word Count, by Gary Provost (paper) $7.95
Pinckert's Practical Grammar, by Robert C. Pinckert $14.95
Teach Yourself to Write, by Evelyn Stenbock (paper) $9.95
The 29 Most Common Writing Mistakes & How to Avoid Them, by Judy Delton $9.95
Writer's Block & How to Use It, by Victoria Nelson $14.95
The Writer's Digest Guide to Manuscript Formats, by Buchman & Groves $16.95
Writer's Encyclopedia, edited by Kirk Polking (paper) $16.95
Writer's Guide to Research, by Lois Horowitz $9.95
Writer's Market, edited by Glenda Neff $21.95
Writing for the Joy of It, by Leonard Knott $11.95

Nonfiction Writing

Basic Magazine Writing, by Barbara Kevles $16.95
How to Sell Every Magazine Article You Write, by Lisa Collier Cool $14.95
How to Write & Sell the 8 Easiest Article Types, by Helene Schellenberg Barnhart $14.95
Writing Creative Nonfiction, by Theodore A. Rees Cheney $15.95
Writing Nonfiction that Sells, by Samm Sinclair Baker $14.95

Fiction Writing

Creating Short Fiction, by Damon Knight (paper) $8.95
Fiction is Folks: How to Create Unforgettable Characters, by Robert Newton Peck (paper) $8.95
Fiction Writer's Help Book, by Maxine Rock $12.95
Fiction Writer's Market, edited by Laurie Henry $18.95
Handbook of Short Story Writing, by Dickson and Smythe (paper) $8.95
How to Write & Sell Your First Novel, by Oscar Collier with Frances Spatz Leighton $14.95
How to Write Short Stories that Sell, by Louise Boggess (paper) $7.95
One Way to Write Your Novel, by Dick Perry (paper) $7.95
Storycrafting, by Paul Darcy Boles (paper) $9.95
Writing the Novel: From Plot to Print, by Lawrence Block (paper) $8.95

Special Interest Writing Books

The Children's Picture Book: How to Write It, How to Sell It, by Ellen E.M. Roberts (paper) $14.95
Comedy Writing Secrets, by Melvin Helitzer $16.95
The Complete Book of Scriptwriting, by J. Michael Straczynski (paper) $9.95
The Complete Guide to Writing Software User Manuals, by Brad M. McGehee (paper) $14.95
The Craft of Comedy Writing, by Sol Saks $14.95
The Craft of Lyric Writing, by Sheila Davis $18.95
Guide to Greeting Card Writing, edited by Larry Sandman (paper) $8.95

How to Make Money Writing About Fitness & Health, by Celia & Thomas Scully $16.95

How to Make Money Writing Fillers, by Connie Emerson (paper) $8.95

How to Sell & Re-Sell Your Writing, by Duane Newcomb $10.95

How to Write a Cookbook and Get It Published, by Sara Pitzer $15.95

How to Write & Sell A Column, by Raskin & Males $10.95

How to Write and Sell (Your Sense of) Humor, by Gene Perret (paper) $9.95

How to Write Tales of Horror, Fantasy & Science Fiction, edited by J.N. Williamson $15.95

How to Write the Story of Your Life, by Frank P. Thomas $14.95

How You Can Make $50,000 a Year as a Nature Photojournalist, by Bill Thomas (paper) $17.95

Mystery Writer's Handbook, by The Mystery Writers of America (paper) $9.95

Nonfiction for Children: How to Write It, How to Sell It, by Ellen E.M. Roberts $16.95

On Being a Poet, by Judson Jerome $14.95

The Poet's Handbook, by Judson Jerome (paper) $8.95

Poet's Market, by Judson Jerome $17.95

Successful Outdoor Writing, by Jack Samson $11.95

Travel Writer's Handbook, by Louise Zobel (paper) $10.95

TV Scriptwriter's Handbook, by Alfred Brenner (paper) $9.95

Writing After 50, by Leonard L. Knott $12.95

Writing for Children & Teenagers, by Lee Wyndham (paper) $9.95

Writing for the Soaps, by Jean Rouverol $14.95

Writing Short Stories for Young People, by George Edward Stanley $15.95

Writing the Modern Mystery, by Barbara Norville $15.95

The Writing Business

A Beginner's Guide to Getting Published, edited by Kirk Polking $10.95

Complete Guide to Self-Publishing, by Tom & Marilyn Ross $19.95

Editing for Print, by Geoffrey Rogers $14.95

Freelance Jobs for Writers, edited by Kirk Polking (paper) $8.95

How to Bulletproof Your Manuscript, by Bruce Henderson $9.95

How to Get Your Book Published, by Herbert W. Bell $15.95

How to Understand and Negotiate a Book Contract or Magazine Agreement, by Richard Balkin $11.95

How to Write Irresistible Query Letters, by Lisa Collier Cool $10.95

How You Can Make $25,000 a Year Writing (No Matter Where You Live), by Nancy Edmonds Hanson $15.95

Literary Agents: How to Get & Work with the Right One for You, by Michael Larsen $9.95

Professional Etiquette for Writers, by William Brohaugh $9.95

To order directly from the publisher, include $2.00 postage and handling for 1 book and 50¢ for each additional book. Allow 30 days for delivery.

Writer's Digest Books, Department B
1507 Dana Avenue, Cincinnati, Ohio 45207
Credit card orders call TOLL-FREE
1-800-543-4644 (Outside Ohio)
1-800-551-0884 (Ohio only)
Prices subject to change without notice.

For information on how to receive Writer's Digest Books at special Book Club member prices, please write to:

Promotion Manager Writer's Digest Book Club
1507 Dana Avenue
Cincinnati, Ohio 45207